Also by Jill Jarnow
THE PATCHWORK POINT OF VIEW
(RE)DO IT YOURSELF

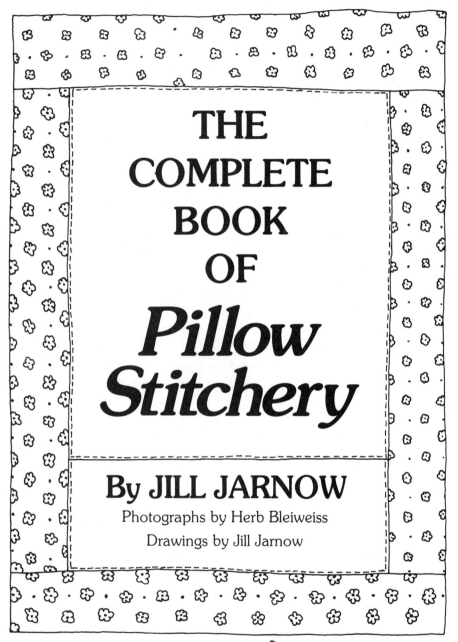

THE
COMPLETE
BOOK
OF
Pillow
Stitchery

By JILL JARNOW

Photographs by Herb Bleiweiss

Drawings by Jill Jarnow

SIMON AND SCHUSTER ✿ NEW YORK

FOR BETSY JARNOW POTTER
who sent us one of her embroidered pillows
for Christmas and started it all

Library of Congress Cataloging in Publication Data

Jarnow, Jill.
    The complete book of pillow stitchery.

    Bibliography: p.
    1. Pillows.   2.   Textile crafts.   I.   Title.
TT410.J37   746.9   78-31232

ISBN 0-671-22538-3

Contents

Acknowledgments

Special thanks to Herb Bleiweiss and Rachel Newman for their fine photography and to Barbara Barnett, Dorothy Globus, Verena Mentzel, Brenda Murphy, Miriam Ress, Vicki Rosenberg, Edie Twining and Melanie Zwerling for sharing their ideas and pillows. Extra thanks to Marlene Connor, editor, for her insight and patience in the face of a Herculean task.

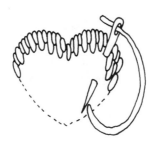

Introduction

Pillows are decorating dynamite. A few well-placed pillows can add the finishing touches of warmth to the furniture in your home. Pillows by themselves can be used as the major elements in an entire decorating (or redecorating) scheme.

In this book you will find an assortment of techniques for decorating pillows. Choose from pillows with embroidery, appliqué, patchwork, quilting, needlepoint, cross stitch or even stencil. Some readers may already be well versed in the techniques presented here but want fresh ideas to go beyond these basic skills, or may want inspiration for new projects. For others, sewing, needlework or other decorative techniques such as stenciling or appliqué may be a completely new experience. Because of this diversity of needs, I have tried to describe each technique in a way that will appeal to the beginner as well as to the expert. There are hand-holding descriptions on how to get started with a new craft, as well as suggestions that might inspire the experienced needleworker to try new ways of designing, stitching and using their creations. Whatever your skills, needs or interest, I hope that you, like me, will soon be inspired by the endlessly wonderful ways there are to use the simple tools and stitches of needlework.

Buying pillows ready-made in department stores or in specialty decorating shops can be depressingly expensive. But, as you will soon see, pillows are surprisingly easy, inexpensive and fun to make at home. Even more important, pillows that you make yourself are so much more exciting and personal than anything mass-produced. Pillows stitched at home can add more to your environment than any other decorative element—bought at any price!

ONE

Positive Points about Pillows

FOR FIRST-TIME STITCHERS

If you are a new sewer or needleworker, a small, manageable pillow is just right for a first project. A simple, two-sided pillow, known as the knife-edge pillow, usually takes no more than a few minutes to construct—even for a beginner. This is also a good choice for the old-time stitcher who likes fast, satisfying projects. For the more adventurous, the pillow top (or front) can be the ideal background for innumerable needlework designs—letting your creativity soar while using your skills and interests.

A basic, plain knife-edge pillow can be stitched and stuffed quickly and easily. To make it more exciting, a colorful patchwork or appliqué top can be made for that pillow in just a few hours, while a needlepoint or embroidered pillow top may take several weeks to complete. Whatever decorating technique you choose, your pillow becomes something very special.

OUT OF THE SCRAP BAG

One of the big pluses about pillow making is that it usually requires such a small amount of materials. Patchwork, appliqué or quilted pillows may be stitched with leftover pieces of other sewing projects. Needlepoint, crewel and cross-stitched pillows may be created with leftover yarn and floss. Even stenciled or painted pillows require minimal amounts of stencil paper and paint. In fact, almost every pillow in this book was assembled from scrap materials.

Aside from the obvious economies of working with leftovers, chances are good that pillows made with these materials will blend with your other needlework projects and will enhance the visual mood you have already established in your home. What could be a more perfect complement to newly sewn curtains or quilts than pillows that utilize some of the same fabrics?

If you have previously been a "kit stitcher" and now have a large assortment of odd ends, this is the perfect way to use up the scraps and step deeper into the world of stitchery. Experiment with those strands of color and get yourself involved with the design aspect of pillow making. You will enjoy your stitchery more than you ever imagined. For help creating your own designs and hints on how to improvise with leftover materials, page 11.

WHAT MATERIALS TO CHOOSE

If you are confused about what materials to choose for a first design project, here are a few hints. After deciding on the technique you plan to use, examine the materials you have tucked away. If you are planning an embroidery or crewel project, lay out potential fabrics and yarns together on a neutral background. To plan patchwork or appliqué, place prospective fabrics and trimmings together on a table or bed in the room where the finished pillow will reside. Or, if the pillow is to be a gift, consider the color feeling in the home of the intended recipient and lay out appropriate materials on a plain surface. Actual color combinations are completely subjective. The photos of the finished pillows should help in planning.

Don't feel compelled to use *just* the materials you already own unless economy is an overriding consideration. Decide what other fabrics or yarns you will need to complete your design idea and make a trip to the local variety store or needlework shop. Don't be dismayed if you find yourself working out a motif based on only one or two colors of yarn or a tiny piece of fabric that is actually from your scrap bag.

Once you have decided on materials, try to approximate the proportions of color and pattern to give yourself an even clearer idea of what your finished design will be like. Arrange, rearrange, add or eliminate. This is what design is all about.

NO SCRAPS? SUPPLIES FOR FIRST-TIMERS

If pillow making is your first venture into sewing or needlework and you haven't already established scrap bags filled with fabrics and yarns, don't despair. Pillows generally require such a minimal amount of materials that the cost of purchasing what you need should be modest. Of course, there are a few economy measures worth consideration.

For a first patchwork, appliqué or quilting project choose moderately priced fabrics like cotton or cotton blend (but not synthetics, because they're hard to work with and don't wear well). Avoid, for the time being, more expensive materials like velvet, wool or silk. Aside from the problem of cost, they will also be hard to handle until you have gained some experience as a needleworker.

For a first needlepoint project, be sure to work on 10-thread-to-the-inch mono needlepoint mesh. The smaller meshes (which are more expensive) take more stitches to the inch and therefore take longer to show results. This can be very disheartening for the beginner.

All the techniques required to make these pillows are easy to learn. And the money you save by not having to pay a professional pillow maker, along with the satisfaction you will get from doing it yourself, should more than compensate for the hour or two it takes to perfect the method. For more on needlepoint, see page 70.

If you are starting your first crewel embroidery, choose a medium-weight tapestry yarn and linen or be prepared to work small. For a first cross-stitch project, chart your design on graph paper first and choose standard embroidery floss and 6- or 8-square-to-the-inch gingham. Later, when you are comfortable with cross stitch, you may want to go on to fine-meshed hardanger cloth and more delicate floss.

The idea is to create something beautiful without having to invest too much time or money, and pillows are the perfect medium. Don't, of course, permanently eliminate the more difficult or time-consuming aspects of stitchery. Wait until you have experience in a particular technique, then refine your skills.

PILLOWS FOR PORTABILITY

Pillow stitchery is perfect for those who like to work on the go. Chart out your plan and assemble your materials at home. Pack everything you need for the project into a small bag. (Don't forget a pair of lightweight scissors!) Carry this bag with you as you travel on a train, bus or plane. Keep this kit bag handy in case you feel like stitching—whether on a break from work during the day, during the evening in front of the television, or just relaxing with a group of close friends.

PILLOWS AND PILLOW KITS FOR PRESENTS

Finished pillows make wonderful gifts for special friends and relatives but—even better—pillow kits that are personally put together make terrific presents for those people who love to work with their hands.

Many experienced stitchers are tired of the commercial kits available in stores but aren't ready to do their own designing. An original design complete with materials and carrying bag will be a special treat with a very personal touch. For friends who have admired your needlework in the past but are timid about getting started themselves, you might assemble a "beginner's kit" complete with a written promise to help them get started stitching.

Special note: For all these kits, you will need to develop appropriate artwork first. For step-by-step instructions on how to do this, see page 10.

Here's what you'll need for each type of kit—whether for your own use or as a gift package:

Patchwork

An overall plan
Cardboard template with pencil
Cotton fabric, or
Precut (at home) cotton pieces
Small needle (between size 6 and 9)
Thread
Thimble
Scissors

Appliqué

The same

Also needed, to be used at home, are press-cloth or towel and an iron.

Needlepoint

Canvas with design drawn in and edges bound with masking tape
Yarn
Needle
Small scissors

Note: To assemble the kit, you will also need a waterproof marker or acrylic paint for transferring the design to the canvas.

Embroidery/Crewel

Linen or cotton fabric with design
Floss or wool
Needle
Small scissors

Note: To assemble the kit, you will also need a pen with waterproof ink and a soft pencil or dressmaker's carbon for transferring the design to the fabric, as described on page 15.

Cross Stitch

Chart of design
Hardanger cloth or gingham fabric
Floss
Needle
Small scissors

Stenciling

Chart of design and description of procedure
Solid color fabric: off-white muslin, solid color cotton, velvet, corduroy
Precut stencils (See page 196 for cutting information.)

Small jars or tubes of acrylic paint, or mix your own special colors with
    acrylic and pack them in clean baby food or other airtight containers.
Sponges

    Pack these materials in a clean plastic shoe box or straw basket from
the dime store or, better yet, a bag of your own design.

PILLOWS WITHOUT NEEDLEWORK

You can quickly make complementary pillows to accompany your most
elaborate creations. A grouping of sophisticated needlework pillows often
looks best when it contains a few simple ones to set them off. Select solid
color fabrics in an appropriate weight and texture from the yard goods
store or use ready-made square and rectangular shapes for these ac-
cents. Choose from today's cotton blend permanent-press items for informal hard-wearing pillows. Another handy suggestion is to use cloth
napkins, dish towels or other household linens; they make great pillow
tops. For a more formal feeling, choose finely embroidered pieces from
the family attic, the local thrift shop or the linen counter of a department
store.

    Scarves also make great pillow covers. They are available in patterns
and styles reflecting a wide range of moods. For informality and whimsy,
use inexpensive bandana neck scarves sold in army-navy stores and in
local variety stores. You can choose from the traditional red or navy or
some of the newer, offbeat greens, pinks and yellows that are now
available.

    On the other end of the scale, you might consider silk, challis and plaid
scarves that are expensive to buy new but often turn up at garage sales
and thrift shops. Add a layer of muslin to the back of any of the more
delicate scarves for strength before stitching them into pillows.

    To make easy and attractive pillows out of any of these materials,
follow the instructions on page 25 for the knife-edge pillow.

    For humorous pillows that children will love making and using, stuff
old clothes. Consider stuffing an outgrown T-shirt or pair of pants or
even stuff and stitch together a group of old socks for pillows like those
described on page 172. For added economy, cut up small pieces of scrap
fabric for the stuffing. Topstitch one end of the garment closed, insert
stuffing and close the remaining seams with hand or machine stitching.

PILLOWS FROM EXISTING NEEDLEWORK

There are many pieces of existing needlework available in craft and museum stores as well as in antique and thrift shops that have great pillow potential. Molas (reverse appliqué pictures) from Guatemala, appliqué from Africa and embroidery from India should all be considered. Choose backing fabrics that blend well with the pillow fronts to make beautiful knife-edge pillows (see page 25).

PILLOWS FROM KNITTING AND CROCHET

If you like to knit or crochet, why not knit or crochet a pillow? Crocheted granny squares (see color section) and any patterned square of knitting can be stitched together like any two-sided knife-edge pillow. For porous stitchery such as granny squares or open-worked knitting, first make and stuff a muslin lining that is the same size as your pillow cover. Topstitch pillow covers, right sides together, with needle and yarn on three sides, insert pillow form and stitch up open side.

COMMERCIAL PILLOW PATTERNS

Pillow stitchery kits have become such a successful industry that pattern companies have decided to get in on the act. As with the packaged pillow kits, the quality of commercial patterns fluctuates from company to company and even from pillow to pillow. For the most part, pillow patterns can be used by you, the pillow designer, as a shortcut to sophisticated, well-designed pillows. But to use pillow patterns to their best advantage, you must also use the ideas and suggested directions in this book. In other words, use the patterns to help with pillow construction but use your own design arrangements, stitch choices and color schemes to create personal pillow tops.

Pillow patterns can be expensive, often costing more than the materials themselves. If you are on a tight budget, avoid spending money on patterns because most pillows can be made at home by even a beginner without the help of a pattern. The pie-wedge pillow on page 127 was done with a commercial pattern although it could have been done easily without one.

PICTURE FRAMES FOR PILLOWS

If, like me, you enjoy making pictures for your pillow covers (rather than overall patterns) you may find picture framing just your thing.

Several Christmases ago, I presented my mother with a 5 x 7 inch needlepoint angel, which I then took back with the promise of returning it as a completed pillow. It sat tucked away in my workbasket for another two Christmases until I'm sure she (and I) had given up hope of ever seeing it again. The problem was that, being such an off-size, it wasn't going to work up into anything very notable. It was too large for a pincushion but too tiny for a throw pillow.

Several weeks ago, when I began my pillow investigations, I remembered this needlepoint. I pulled it out of the basket and reblocked it (see page 81). As it was drying, I began considering how to enlarge the surface. Of course I could have added additional mesh to the outside and extended the stitching, but I wanted to try something a little more adventurous. I decided to make a patchwork frame out of wide gingham ribbon, using the patchwork procedure on page 119. When the ribbon was attached, I pinned additional ribbon and lace around the outside and machine-stitched them down. I backed the pillow with blue velveteen. When I was done, I had made a 10 x 12¼ inch pillow from a 6 x 8 inch needlepoint and, although it wasn't Christmas, I presented the finished piece to its rightful owner. For more on the needlepoint angel pillow, see page 92.

By the way, I was unhappy with the machine stitching because it had too much "presence" on the ribbon and lace. When making a later "picture" with lace, I did all decorative stitching by hand and was much more satisfied with the results.

Since the completion of that first angel pillow I have experimented with framing other types of picture pillows. The lace appliqué pillow on page 162 is framed with striped fabric and yellow lacy trim. The crewel embroidery cat on page 53 is also framed.

Special note for the experienced: If you have been an avid needlepointer or an embroidery maven for several years but have never finished your own pillows you have probably been spending exorbitant amounts having your needlework blocked and stitched into a pillow. Or, even worse, you have a drawer full of finished needlework waiting for the day when your budget can support a trip to the needlework shop or upholsterer for finishing. You've probably never considered doing the job yourself. After all, a finished pillow looks so impressive.

Take it from me, if you were clever enough to complete the needlework, you're smart enough to finish the pillow. For special information on blocking and finishing needlework pillows, see page 81.

TWO

Designing Your Own Needlework Pillows

Many accomplished needleworkers are devout kit users. Convenience is the major factor in repeated purchases of needlework kits because the package usually contains everything needed for the completion of a project with a minimum of fuss. Unfortunately, when you are finished you have a creation that could have been done (and probably was) by several thousand other people. In addition, you may even be less than satisfied with your pillow if it looks radically different from the picture on the package.

Needlework pillow kits have become so popular it's easy to forget that needlework can and should be a work of personal expression.

I am not downgrading the use of all kits because there are many excellent ones on the market. I am, however, objecting to the constant and habitual use of commercially prepared needlework. Most people don't realize that they *can* design their own needlepoint, embroidery, patchwork, appliqué or quilted pillows, and, in so doing, they will add an exciting new dimension to their needlework and to their lives. Any needleworker interested enough to read a book about pillows has enough interest and spirit of adventure to step beyond convenient needlework into the realm of personal creation. It's not as hard as it seems, and it's not even necessary to be able to draw (often an excuse). In addition, assembling your own good-quality designs and materials is so economical you'll be amazed at the savings.

9

For a breakdown of what materials you will need for each technique, see page 4 and the introductions to each appropriate chapter.

BUILDING UP THE COURAGE

How many times have you looked at a finished needlework pillow in a needlework shop or magazine and said "I can do that!" But then you felt the same insecurities that many people feel. What do I do? How do I begin? Well, help is here.

On the following pages you will find everything you need to know to get started creating your own needlework. One special note: I can point you in the right direction, but only by putting my advice to use will you develop your skills and confidence. Don't be afraid to make mistakes. Reject something if it doesn't turn out the way you expected. Even for experienced designers, devising satisfactory artwork can take several tries.

FINDING ARTWORK TO HELP
YOUR DESIGN IDEAS

Pillow stitchery design does not require drawing anything from scratch (unless, of course, you want to). Tracing a shape from a reference book or any other source and arranging what you have traced into a pleasing composition definitely counts as creating your own artwork. The most sophisticated craftspeople and designers (including kit designers) do it all the time. The trick is in knowing what to choose and how to use what you have traced. That's what creativity is all about. Even if you can't draw a straight line (and who really can, after all?), you can create exciting, original pillows.

There are countless sources to consult for tracing material. The most obvious place is this book. I have given drawings and charts as well as descriptions of the development of each pillow to make your own stitchery easier. For the most part I worked with scrap materials, as did the other people who contributed to this book, so chances are good that you will not be able to duplicate our pillows exactly. But don't be disappointed or frustrated by this. Our designs are here for you to use but it is our intention that you add your own touches to each project.

There are other craft books in bookstores and libraries with artwork appropriate for tracing as well as books that are intended to be used primarily as picture sources. Dover is the biggest publisher of these books, which have been printed with the intention that artists and designers will use them to trace motifs. Many of these books are reprints from old, once out-of-print manuals and they are invaluable for needlework ideas. They cover a huge range of subjects from the folk art of many countries to Victorian and Art Nouveau designs as well as cross-stitch and stencil patterns. Soft-cover and inexpensive, they are widely available. For an unbelievable list of what is in print, write directly to Dover Publications Inc., 180 Varick Street, New York, N.Y. 10014.

The next place to turn for tracing material is to picture books. Use pictures of birds, flowers or animals from nature handbooks. Consider pictures from children's magazines and storybooks as well as travel and architecture books. Greeting cards, seed catalogues, posters and magazine advertisements can all be transformed into images on pillows.

Don't forget the countless wonderful craft magazines that are now available in local shops. If you live near a store that carries foreign periodicals such as Rizzoli, 712 Fifth Avenue in New York City, take time to browse through the French, Italian and German craft magazines for a different slant on pillow crafts.

CHOOSING A NEEDLEWORK TECHNIQUE

Choose a technique for making a pillow top according to what you enjoy doing or what you would like to learn to do. Don't be afraid to try a technique for the first time; most of the pillow projects described in this collection are easy enough for a beginner. To get started, read through the appropriate introductory chapter to learn about materials, procedures and special qualities of the technique.

MAKING DECISIONS

The best way to zero in on a pillow project is to decide where the finished pillow will be used. If the pillow is for your living room couch, make your choices according to the color and feeling already in that room or that will complement the couch. When working with scrap materials (as with so many of the pillows in this book) lay out the materials you intend to use in the area where the finished pillow will be. You should then get a clearer picture of what to add or eliminate. If you are purchasing materials especially for an area—say, to match new curtains—it helps to have a swatch of fabric with you when you make your purchases. If you have no samples available, be inventive. Try to find among the things in your home a scarf, a blouse, an ashtray, a vase or anything else in colors that seem right for the area you are decorating. Take this color reference with you to the store because it is very hard to remember clearly colors or shades, especially when confronted with the avalanche of materials in a yard goods shop. You'll be glad for the help when it comes time to make a decision.

In addition, let the objects around you at home suggest designs for pillows. A rug, a picture, a piece of china or another pillow might be just the inspiration you need. If the pillow is a gift for someone, try to apply the same principles.

DESIGN BY ARRANGEMENT

In most cases it is best to decide first what size you want your pillow and adjust your artwork accordingly. If you are designing an appliqué pillow using leftover materials such as pieces of lace or crochet (as in the lace landscape on page 161), you may have to lay out your materials in position and let this dictate the size of the pillow. Small pieces of needle-work (such as the needlepoint angel on page 92) can be made larger with the addition of a patchwork frame.

If you are working with embroidery, needlepoint or stencil you will be able to decide in the beginning what size your pillow is to be. If you are working with scraps, the available canvas mesh or backing fabric will dictate certain restrictions.

Take all of these variables into consideration and decide on the dimensions of your pillow. Using a pencil and ruler, draw an outline of your pillow on layout bond or tracing paper, which is available in art supply stores. To square the corners, use a book as a template.

Assemble the picture elements that you want to use in your design by tracing them from the source onto separate pieces of transparent paper with a dark pencil or pen. If they have to be enlarged or reduced, see page 16.

On a clear surface, lay your design tracings on top of each other, smoothing them flat with the side of your hand so one shows through another. Shift them around until you think you have a pleasing arrangement. Next, place the outline of the pillow on top of these pieces and smooth it out so all of the elements are visible within its boundaries. This job will be easier if you use lightweight paper and work on a light-colored surface. If the artwork is too hard to see, try taping your pieces on a well-lighted window during the day. A light table, which is a piece of frosted glass or plastic with a light under it, is also excellent. If you decide early on the position of a major element you can hold this in position with a piece of tape while you experiment with the placement of the other elements.

Getting the right combination of design elements and placement of these pieces can take time, so expect to work by trial and error. You may want to trace a rabbit shape from a natural history book or magazine and a border design from a Dover reprint. It may take several tries to find a border with the right flavor. You might want to experiment with the size of the rabbit. You may even find that you want to adjust the size of the pillow to accommodate your design elements. Trial and error is the only way to create a satisfying design.

CHOOSING MATERIALS, STITCHES
AND COLORS

Once you have your design on paper, you will have to choose the materials, colors and stitching that will make it come to life. This too will be a trial-and-error process.

For beginners there is only one word of precaution: simplicity. Until you have a working knowledge of the strengths and weaknesses of a technique, stick to simple, straightforward shapes. Avoid trying to make a technique do something that it can't. If you want pictorial detail, choose embroidery; for more simplified or geometric shapes, choose patchwork or crazy quilting.

Remember, materials have their strong points as well as their limitations. For charm and informality, choose delicate, printed cotton; but for sophistication you might use velvet, silk or challis. If you back a needlepoint pillow with silk, it will be formal; back it with corduroy and it will be rustic. Whatever your choice, start slowly. Nothing in this book is difficult, but all new skills take practice.

Assemble all of your intended materials together and lay them out on a clean surface according to your design plan. Eliminate and add until you are satisfied with the overall color and texture. Each technique will have its own dimensions to consider and sometimes you just can't predict how two materials will look stitched together or how two stitches will look next to each other. If you feel that you have developed some interesting combinations but you've never actually seen them together in a finished pillow, try them out. With patchwork or appliqué you can pin or baste your materials into position before doing the final stitching. Embroidery is generally easy to remove, but do it carefully. Needlepoint can be the most difficult to correct although this is one technique that is particularly open for experimentation. I have found myself removing colors and stitches over and over on the same piece of needlepoint, which can be annoying and time-consuming. On the other hand, needlepoint wears so well and is so pleasing to look at that it is worth working on a design until it is right.

Above all, remember that experimentation and revision are an ongoing part of the creative process. Your morale might sink a bit after your third attempt to get the combinations just the way you want them. When this happens, it's time for a little outside help. Turn again to your craft books and magazines and look at examples of the technique you are struggling with. You might see a color or stitch combination that will solve your problem. Or, return to the source your inspiration—the couch, the rug, the scarf or the tea cup—and look to see what subtle colors are included in the overall color makeup. You may discover that there is an off-beat color that permeates the whole design or highlights a small area. Don't be afraid to be daring with your color if it gives your work the spice it needs.

TRANSFERRING A DESIGN

When your design is set and you have gathered your materials you are ready to prepare your fabric for stitching. The information that follows is basic and general. For specifics see the introductions to each technique.

Always work on a hard surface. If a table top isn't available, use the floor. It is very important to keep your materials as flat as possible by smoothing out any bulges in the paper that your artwork is on with the side of your hand. Iron out any wrinkles in fabric, if needed.

For embroidery, secure the fabric that will receive the pattern face up with masking tape. Tape the artwork face up over this with the tape running along one side, as shown. Place dressmaker's carbon, in a color that will be visible on the fabric receiving the transfer, face down between the artwork and the fabric. Carefully trace around the design, using a hard pencil or tracing wheel. You can also use graphite carbon for this

*Transferring a design: (from the bottom up) fabric (face up),
dressmaker's carbon (face down), artwork (face up)*

but try to avoid using standard carbon because it will smear on the fabric.
You can also use chalk by rubbing it on the back of the artwork. Tape
the artwork to the fabric to receive the design and trace with a hard
pencil. Once this is done, remove the artwork and trace over the chalk
lines with a pencil so the design will be visible when the chalk rubs off.

Another method is to trace the outline of your design through the back
of the paper with a soft pencil, tape this to the fabric face up and retrace
over the lines to transfer the pencil lines to the fabric.

If the fabric you are using is transparent, place it over the artwork and
trace it right through. If your fabric is lightweight, tape the design to a
well-lighted window with the fabric over it and trace with a pencil.

If the fabric you have chosen is too rough for any of these methods,
there is still another approach. Trace your design on tissue paper. Baste
this, drawing side up, in position on the fabric. Use the lines of this tracing
as a stitch guide and embroider right through the tissue into the base
fabric. When the embroidery is complete, or as the paper starts to get in
the way, carefully pull away the tissue paper.

For patchwork, appliqué and quilting you will need to make templates. Shirt cardboard is best although lightweight board such as oaktag or index cards will also work. Transfer the design to the cardboard with carbon paper and cut it out with a small utility knife, single-edged razor blade or scissors. Trace the template to fabric with a pencil or tailor's chalk. When doing patchwork, trace the template to the wrong side of the fabric; for appliqué, trace onto the right side.

Transfer needlepoint designs to canvas by tracing directly through the mesh. Darken the lines on the artwork so they are visible, tape the canvas securely over the artwork and trace, using a permanent felt-tipped marker or acrylic paint.

ENLARGING A PICTURE

When you find a picture in a book or magazine that you would like to use in a pillow design you will probably have to enlarge it to the right size. Occasionally you will have to reduce it.

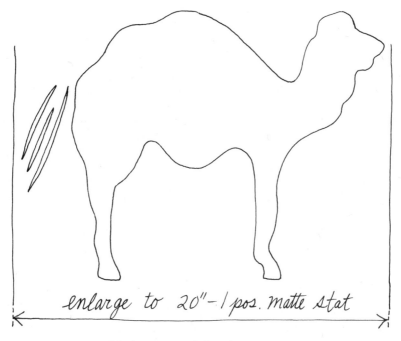

Marking artwork for photostating

Method 1: Mechanically

The easiest way to change the size of a picture is to photostat the artwork. This is a method rarely mentioned in craft books and magazines probably because it requires some footwork, might take overnight and can be expensive. It is, however, the easiest and most accurate way to get the job done. Look in the phone book for a photostat service near you. Call and find out how long it takes to get your stats and the prices for various sizes. This way you can decide ahead of time whether you want to invest.

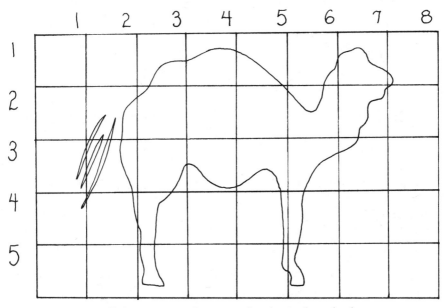

Enlarging or reducing art by the grid method

Artwork to be photostated should be drawn or traced on white paper with dark black lines. Decide how much of an enlargement (or reduction) you want and indicate this clearly near the drawing. Mark one extreme of the drawing, as shown, with the new dimension that you want. You will not be able to change the proportion of the artwork so if you enlarge the 3-inch side of a 3 x 4 inch drawing to 12 inches, the 4-inch side will automatically enlarge to 16 inches. So decide whether the height or width is the more crucial dimension for your purposes and order your enlargement accordingly.

Order a positive, matte-finish photostat. This is the economy variety and it isn't very glamorous. Don't be put off if it arrives covered with splotches and dust. If the lines of the artwork are clear, that's really all you need.

Artwork enlarged beyond 16 x 20 inches usually arrives in pieces or pieced. Match up the lines, tape the paper together and proceed with your project.

Some photostat houses will give same-day service, others take overnight or a few days, so be sure to double check when you call.

If you have access to an opaque projector, through a school or library, you are in luck. Ask someone how to use it. Tape a piece of paper on the wall or screen, focus your artwork to the right size and trace.

Method 2: By Hand

The simplest method for enlarging artwork at home is to use corresponding grids. Trace your artwork onto graph paper or unlined paper. If using unlined paper, use a ruler to draw a grid of equal-size squares right over your picture. Number the boxes across the top and down the side, as shown.

Next, on another piece of paper draw a larger grid with larger squares. Again, if you have a large sheet of graph paper the job will be easier. If you want the enlargement to be four times the size of the original, the new grid must contain boxes that are four times larger than those in the smaller grid. The new grid must contain the same number of squares as the original and must be numbered the same way.

Mark off with a dot in the same location on the larger grid, each place where a line crosses the smaller grid. When all of these locations are marked, connect the dots. Be sure to keep the original handy for reference. When all the dots are connected, your enlargement is complete.

To reduce a pattern, simply reverse the procedure. Make a grid of smaller squares and mark off the artwork square by square.

A CHECKLIST FOR EVERY NEEDLEWORKER

Whether you are a beginner at needlework and sewing or a long-established stitcher interested in broadening your design horizons, the pillow projects in this book are meant to be appealingly uncomplicated. However, it's not unusual to find that by merely taking a few so-called shortcuts you can make an easy project difficult. Whenever I catch myself cutting corners, I try to remind myself of the possible dangers. Usually I can get on the right track before disaster strikes.

The following list contains a number of good practice reminders to help yourself avoid calamity.

1. Always use sharp scissors or shears for cutting fabric, especially for patchwork and appliqué.
2. Keep a workbasket handy with needles, straight pins, dressmaker's chalk, tape measure, small scissors, an assortment of thread colors and any other supplies that you find yourself using repeatedly.
3. When sewing or drawing, work on a flat, clean, hard surface. If nothing else is available, try the floor.
4. Choose the right tool for the job. If necessary, experiment and do research until you find the tool that works. Use a large, blunt needle for needlepoint and a sharp, fine one for quilting. Mark on fabric with dressmaker's carbon, chalk or a soft pencil. For needlepoint, always use a waterproof marker when drawing a design on canvas.
5. Use materials that are clean and durable. Avoid fabrics or yarns that are stained or worn. Stitching them into needlework will not improve their appearance.
6. Press all fabrics free of wrinkles before including them in a pillow project, including the fabrics for pillow backs. Although needlepoint mesh should not be pressed before being stitched, finished needlepoint stitchery must be blocked before being turned into a pillow.
7. Realistically appraise your attention span. If you like instant results, choose those pillow projects that have been specially noted for their speed. If you are patient and methodical, consider the long-range projects such as needlepoint or cross stitch.
8. Neatness counts. Sloppy work interferes with the overall impact and success of your needlework. Although each person has a different style (some people make small, even stitches, others stitch in large, bold strokes), loose threads and frayed edges should not punctuate your stitchery.
9. If you come to an impasse, whether technical or artistic, look for help. If you have friends or relatives who are enthusiastic needleworkers, you might turn to them for advice, direction or reassurance. If no one is available, read through craft books and magazines in bookshops and libraries for new approaches and ideas. Look at finished pieces of needlework in boutiques and museums to see how the stitchery has been done.

THREE

Pillow Fillings
and Construction

The pillows presented in this collection are, for the most part, made up of two basic pieces—the decorative pillow top and the plain, durable pillow back. Most of us, contributors and readers alike, enjoy doing one form of needlework or another and are looking for straightforward, uncomplicated ways of turning our stitchery into decorative home accessories. Therefore, 90 percent of the pillows described on the following pages are stitched in the most basic pillow shape—the two-sided knife-edge pillow. A few pillows are variations of the knife edge with ruffles or lace added in the seams. Some have diagonal stitching across the corners for a more boxy effect. Even the oversized rainbow mat on page 136 is a variation of the knife-edge construction.

A few pillows have been done in a slightly more involved box construction and a sprinkling have been done in free-form shapes such as the sock pillows on page 172, but even these were chosen because, aside from being attractive, they are easy to create.

I prefer the look of the pure knife-edge pillow and you may too. On the other hand, if your tastes run to any of the other constructions given here, don't be afraid to combine elements to create the look you enjoy. This is a book about improvisation and personal choice—so go ahead and transform a knife-edge needlepoint pillow into a box-constructed pillow.

In addition, most of the pillows in this collection have no interlinings and are hand stitched shut rather than having zippers. This, too, was a personal decision made to fit my own temperament, life style and taste. I find zippers bulky and unattractive and I rarely have the patience to put them in. I have been satisfied to remove the hand stitching where the pillow was closed, take out the stuffing to clean or wash the pillow and then replace the stuffing, hand stitching the pillow closed again.

Sad to say, if well used, pillows don't last forever (except, perhaps, needlepoint pillows, and even they can need new backing fabric after a few years). If I wash or clean a pillow three times during its life, that's a lot. So I prefer not to use zippers in my pillows.

Some readers may not agree with this attitude. Vicki Rosenberg, who stitched the sampler (page 61) and the crewel flower basket (page 56), includes interlining and zippers in all of her pillows. You may want to do this also. For more on zippers, see page 32.

Pillow Density

Pillows should be inviting to look at and pleasant to use, but pillow density is a matter of personal preference. I prefer my pillows to be firm enough to hold their shape but not so tightly filled as to be rocklike. A loosely packed pillow won't hold its shape and will need to be fluffed up often; a pillow that is too dense will pull at the seams.

The best way to learn your preference, no matter which filling you use, is to experiment. Stuff your pillow and live with it for a few days. You will soon see whether your pillow needs more or less stuffing or whether your initial impulse was correct. To make changes, open up the small hand stitches, add to or take out stuffing and sew the seam up again.

FILLINGS FOR PILLOWS

Most of the pillows included in this collection are stuffed with Dacron or polyester fiberfill. A few, such as the Turkish cushion and Turkish bolster, are made with ready-made forms. In the following section, I have compiled a list of pillow stuffings. I have noted those that work particularly well and I have indicated those that have proved unsatisfactory. In general, Dacron is the most desirable pillow stuffing, but because it is so expensive, it is sometimes necessary to use an alternative material.

Loose Fillings

Dacron or polyester fiberfill, available in one-pound bags in variety stores, sewing supply shops and department stores, is light, resilient and easy to pack into pillows. A clean and nonallergenic synthetic, it is an ideal pillow stuffing. I use fiberfill for all small pillow projects, but for giant pillows I have occasionally had to turn to other stuffings. In large amounts, Dacron can be prohibitively expensive.

Special note on Dacron quilt batting: When buying Dacron fiberfill, read the label carefully to make sure you are getting pillow stuffing. Dacron batting, meant for quilts, comes pressed in large, flat sheets. This is the same Dacron sold loosely in bags but it is more expensive. You'll be spending more than necessary if you buy quilt batting and tear it apart for pillows. On the other hand, if you have small scraps of batting left over from a quilt project, it makes sense to cut or tear it apart into small pieces for pillows.

Kapok, also available by the bag in sewing supply stores and in some variety stores, is a vegetable product. Less expensive than Dacron, kapok is excellent for stuffing large pillows. Easy to handle, it is denser than Dacron. Pillows stuffed with kapok are considerably heavier than those stuffed with fiberfill. Kapok tends to be lumpy so be sure to fluff it carefully before stuffing it into a pillow. Kapok-filled pillows are not as resilient as those filled with Dacron and they may have to be dismantled and fluffed occasionally.

Foam chips are also widely available by the bag in sewing supply stores. They are inexpensive but I don't recommend them as an entirely satisfactory pillow stuffing. First, they are hard to handle. Filled with static electricity, they would rather stick to you or your clothing than be coaxed into a pillow. Once inside the pillow, they give a cold, unpleasant texture. Yet, because of their low price you might consider foam chips for filling oversized pillows, particularly if you are making them for a play area to be used by children and pets.

For ease in filling a large pillow, consider placing the entire plastic package inside the completed pillow cover. Carefully pierce the plastic wrapper so the chips can move freely inside the pillow. Add additional foam chips by hand, if necessary, until the pillow is full. If the pillow fabric is thin, such as lightweight Indian throw cloth (which makes attractive floor pillows), gently draw out the plastic wrapping. If the pillow fabric is heavy, you may be able to get away with leaving the plastic wrapper inside.

Styrofoam pellets are in the same category as foam chips: inexpensive to buy, hard to insert, and coarse in texture. You won't want to use these pellets to fill a needlepoint pillow but they are wonderful in large pillows. Styrofoam pellets will give a pillow a bean bag effect that children will enjoy. Again, these pellets are difficult to coax into a pillow so consider using the same method recommended for foam chips.

Surgical cotton or cotton balls might be a handy choice if you are looking around the house on a rainy afternoon for something to stuff a small pillow, although for anything larger than a pincushion this can be very expensive. Don't go out to buy this cotton as a pillow filling. Fiberfill is better in almost every way. I am 100 percent in favor of using natural fibers for pillow tops (in fact, I am almost fanatical about it) but I have become equally devoted to synthetics for pillow fillings.

Goose down is used by many professional upholsterers to fill pillows. It is not readily available in retail stores; I have never used it. I understand that it is costly and difficult to use without special equipment. Feathers, like foam chips, tend to fly around the room. In addition, pillows filled completely with down need to be fluffed into shape often, and many people are allergic to it.
Down is much better as a pillow stuffing when used in combination with Dacron. Information about down and Dacron ready-made pillow forms is in the section that follows.

Fabric scraps from old cotton clothing and from other sewing projects can also be used for stuffing pillows. For best results, cut your scraps into tiny pieces and make sure to pack your pillow tightly; fabric stuffings tend to flatten easily.

Old nylon stockings and pantyhose make fine pillow stuffing when cut into tiny pieces. Be sure to cut off and discard any elastic before using and pack the small pieces of nylon firmly and generously inside the pillow.

Stuffing a Pillow with Dacron or Other Loose Filling

To use fiberfill, first prepare the pillow as described in this book, leaving a 2- to 3-inch opening in the stitching on one side. Turn the pillow right side out and gently free the corners with a large crochet hook or other long, blunt instrument.

Pull a handful of fiberfill from the plastic bag in which it is packed and tear it gently into fist-sized pieces. Push these balls one at a time through the opening at the side of the pillow and into the two farthest corners. For very small pillows, the pieces should be closer to the size of cotton balls.

When the two corners are packed (you may have to use the crochet hook to push the filling in place), continue packing small amounts of fiberfill into the pillow until it is firmly filled. Before stuffing the pillow completely, guide several handfuls of Dacron into the two remaining corners, using the crochet hook if necessary. Continue to add stuffing until the pillow is full. Turn in the raw edge of the opening, pin it in place with straight pins and stitch it shut with small hem stitches.

READY-MADE PILLOW FORMS

Dacron forms are now available in sewing supply stores and make excellent pillow fillings if you plan to make standard-size pillows. However, for improvised shapes and sizes it is best to stuff your pillows with loose Dacron as described earlier.

Dacron- and down-stuffed pillow forms are available in better sewing shops and department stores. At full price, these forms can be expensive, but I have found that they are often included in the biannual white sales that have become department store tradition. Watch for these sales and buy when the price is right.

Foam forms make rigid, strong pillow fillings, ideal for projects like the backgammon pillow on page 165. Available in sheets and geometric forms in many sewing supply shops, they can be ordered in specific sizes and shapes from stores specializing in foam. See the Yellow Pages of your phone book for listings in your area. To cut foam, use a sharp mat knife or scissors.

Use foam forms for special purpose pillows and mats, but for luxurious, decorative throws, use a softer filling.

Ready-made kapok forms are also available in certain sewing supply shops, which will sometimes make them to size. Believe it or not, this can be an economical way to stuff a large pillow. Many shops buy filling in enough quantity to bring down the price even with the additional charge for fabricating the pillow form, thus a custom-made form may cost considerably less than the materials bought in small quantities. Shop around in your neighborhood to see what's available.

Covering Ready-made Pillow Forms

For instructions on how to cover a ready-made pillow form, see section on knife-edge pillows, below.

PILLOW CONSTRUCTION

There are two basic pillow types—the knife edge and the box edge. There are many ways to interpret each, and both constructions can be used to create almost any shape. The knife edge is easiest, and, as I have already mentioned, I prefer it. As you browse through this book, you will see that I have used this construction to create all kinds of pillows—large, small, round, oblong, person-shaped and tree-shaped!

KNIFE-EDGE PILLOWS

Method 1: Covering a Pillow Form

Measure across the width of your pillow form from seam to seam, keeping your tape measure taut. Measure the height in this way also.

Using a pencil and ruler, line off these dimensions on two pieces of fabric, right sides down. Wherever possible, draw along the straight grain

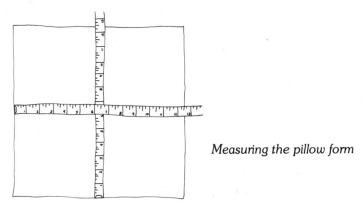

Measuring the pillow form

Knife-edge pillow construction:

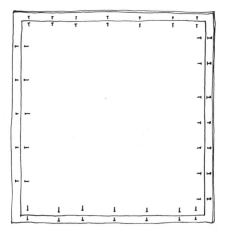

1. *Pin fabrics face to face.*

2. *Stitch around all four corners (leaving an opening for reversing pillow).*

of the fabric. Or, line off the dimensions on a sheet of paper, cut out and trace the shape onto the surface of the fabric. Cut out the fabric ¼ inch from the drawn lines on all sides to allow for seams.

Place fabric pieces right sides together so all edges are even and pin together firmly (see drawing 1). Stitch together along drawn seam line ¼ inch from edge of fabric. Begin stitching near one corner and stitch around sides to include all corners. This may be done by hand, but for the strength of your pillow machine stitching is best.

Leave a large opening on one edge for inserting the pillow form (preferably the bottom if your pillow design indicates one). For strength, backstitch at the beginning and end of this stitching (see drawing 2).

Remove pins and clip the pillow corners on the diagonal with sharp scissors. Do this about ⅛ inch above the stitching and not through it (see drawing 3).

Turn the pillow right side out and gently free the corners with a large crochet hook or other blunt instrument.

Insert the pillow form and fold in the seam allowance of the remaining opening so it blends with the seam that is already sewn. Pin it in place and hand stitch closed. Use either tiny overhand stitches or blind stitches that are hidden in the seam (see drawing 4).

Method 2: The Improvised Knife-edge Pillow

From time to time, you may want to design and stitch your pillow top first and worry about its dimensions later. You may inadvertently design

3. *Clip corners; turn pillow cover right side out and insert pillow form.*

4. *Pin the opening closed and stitch shut.*

a standard size pillow but most likely you will come up with a very personal, nonconforming pillow top.

Once your pillow top is complete, decide where the boundaries are to be and line these off on the wrong side of the fabric with a pencil and ruler. You may have to tape your creation to a sunny window to see the design on the back of the fabric. In the case of stitchery done on velvet or other opaque material, line off the pillow dimensions on the front of the design with a ruler and dressmaker's chalk and transfer these lines to the back by placing the design, face up, over dressmaker's carbon, also face up, and marking over the boundaries with a tracing wheel. Be sure to choose a color of dressmaker's carbon that will be visible on your fabric and press firmly on the wheel as you trace for a clear transfer.

Trim away excess fabric, leaving ¼-inch seam allowance on all sides. Select a backing fabric and trim this to the same size as the pillow front. Pin the pillow front and back together face to face and stitch as described in the previous section.

Stuff the pillow with Dacron fiberfill or other loose stuffing (see page 22) and stitch closed.

The Modified Box Pillow
(Made from a Knife-edge Pillow)

For a soft-looking box pillow such as the Turkish cushion on page 34 or the rainbow bolster on page 136, consider the modified box.

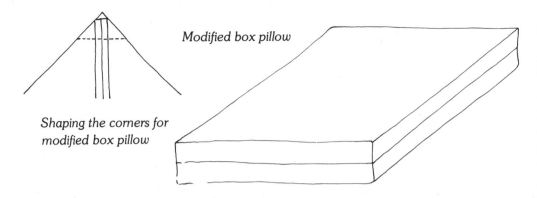

Shaping the corners for modified box pillow

Modified box pillow

Construct the pillow according to the knife-edge construction. Stitch the outside edge as directed, but before reversing the pillow into its permanent position, shape the corners. Fold each corner, one at a time, so the side seam is centered. Draw a line with a pencil and ruler diagonally across the corner as shown, press and pin. Stitch across the line and backstitch for strength. Cut off the excess fabric ½ inch from the stitch line. Repeat this on all sides, turn pillow right sides out, stuff and stitch closed.

Turkish Corners

For a special effect, add a row of hand stitching just above the modified box stitching and pull to form gathers. Tie off each end, reverse pillow and stuff.

The Pillow Seam Opening

When using a pillow form you will have to leave a large opening in one seam of the pillow top so the form will slip into it easily. If you are going to stuff your pillow with loose filling, this opening can be just large enough for comfortably reversing the pillow. The best size for this will be dictated by the weight of the fabrics involved. Needlepoint is bulky and will require a large hole for reversing, while cotton patchwork and appliqué are lightweight and will easily fit through a smaller opening. If you intend to use a pillow form you will need to leave almost an entire side open but, wherever possible, include all corners in your construction stitching.

Clipping Curves

When making round pillows or shaped pillows that include curves, you will have to clip away fabric from these curves before reversing the pillow to eliminate tension and avoid possible puckers. To do this, clip up to, but not through, the stitching, as shown.

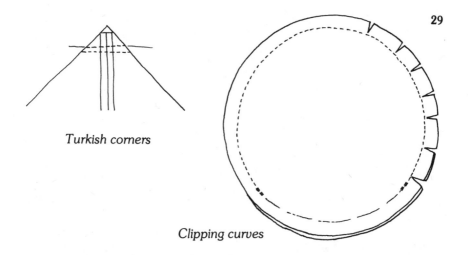

Turkish corners

Clipping curves

Unusual Shapes

You can construct any shape of pillow front into a knife-edge pillow using the same method. Transfer the boundary lines of the pillow design to the back of the fabric, place the fabric face to face with a backing fabric and stitch along the drawn outline. Trim away excess material. Leave an opening large enough to reverse the pillow comfortably, stuff and stitch closed.

BOX-EDGE PILLOWS

The box-edge pillow is made up of a top and a bottom section, which are joined together by a length of fabric called a "boxing strip." The ribbon pillow on page 158 is constructed with this method as is the needlepoint pillow on page 95. If you are new at pillow stitchery, try making a ribbon box or other lightweight box pillow before going on to the bulky and more difficult needlepoint box.

The Traditional Box

To make a box pillow, first determine the size of the pillow front. This will also be the dimension for the pillow back. For the length of the boxing, add up the dimensions of the perimeter of the front (add an inch or two for seam allowance). The width of the boxing strip will depend on the thickness of the form you are covering or, if you are stuffing the pillow with loose filling later, your personal preference.

Traditional box pillow construction:

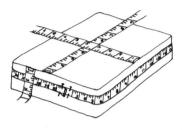

*Measuring to make
a traditional box pillow*

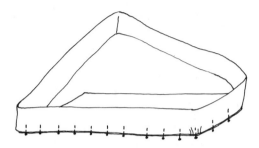

*1. Pin one edge of the boxing strip
face-to-face with pillow front.*

Draw the boxing strip on the wrong side of the fabric with a pencil and ruler according to the measurements you have chosen and cut out ¼ inch from the drawn line on all sides.

Stitch the ends of the boxing strip together by pinning them face to face and sewing along the seam allowance.

Pin one edge of the boxing strip face to face with the pillow front, easing the boxing around any corners. Stitch in place on the drawn stitching lines.

Pin the pillow back to the remaining half of the boxing strip in the same manner and stitch in place, leaving a large enough seam opening to reverse and stuff the pillow. Clip the boxing corners to ease tension, reverse the pillow, stuff and stitch closed.

Circular Box Pillows

Make circular box pillows using the same method. Measure the perimeter of the circular top to determine the length of the box strip. Choose the width according to the thickness of the form to be covered or by personal preference. Draft this shape on the wrong side of your chosen fabric with pencil and ruler. Cut it out, leaving a ¼-inch seam allowance on all sides. Pin the boxing strip face to face with the circular front, ease around the curves and pin in place. Use the pin method of registration suggested for patchwork on page 123 for accuracy.

Stitch boxing strip in place and add the backing fabric, using the same method. Before reversing the pillow, clip the seams on both edges of the boxing to relieve tension.

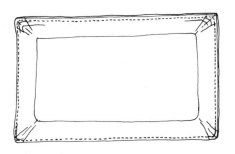

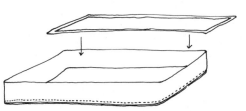

3. *Pin pillow back to remaining half of boxing strip in same manner. Stitch, leaving opening for reversing pillow. Reverse, stuff, stitch closed.*

2. *Stitch in place on all sides.*

Patchwork Box Pillow

A second way to create a rectangular or square box pillow is to use patchwork strips. The backgammon pillow on page 165 and the crewel flower basket on page 56 were both done with this method.

When your pillow top is complete, add a strip of fabric to each side in a coordinating fabric. Each strip should be the same length as the side to which it is being sewn plus ¼-inch seam allowance on all sides. The depth of the strips will be a matter of personal choice. Attach as you would any patchwork addition by pinning and stitching the strips face to face with the pillow front.

Form the corners by pinning together the seam allowances face to face at each corner and stitching.

The pillow back will be the same measurements as the pillow front. Pin and stitch this face to face with the remaining edges of the patchwork strips as you would for any box pillow.

REMOVABLE PILLOW COVERS

Lap Backs for Knife-edge and Box-edge Pillows

If you are using a pillow form and intend to remove it from its cover often, you may want to make a lap-back cover. This is made of two overlapping sections of fabric. It is easy to make and, in my opinion, is the best solution for making removable cases. It is ideal for a pillow that sits on a bed by day and is used for sleeping at night.

Prepare the pillow top with the stitchery of your choice. To make the back, measure the height and width of the pillow top. Cut two pieces of

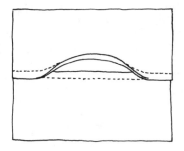

Make lap backs for removable pillow covers.

fabric the same width as the pillow top (plus seam allowance) with height measuring half that of the pillow top plus an extra 3½ inches on each.

Turn under the center edges of each half and press to form a ½-inch hem. Turn the pressed edges under one inch more, press, and pin to form a 1½-inch hem. Stitch in place with a straight stitch, making sure to catch the edge of the hem in the stitching. Repeat this on the second half.

Place these two pieces face to face with the pillow front so the hemmed edges overlap slightly. Pin them together securely and stitch on all four sides. Make diagonal clips in the corners, reverse the pillow, free the corners with a crochet hook and carefully insert pillow form.

Zippers?

Items of clothing such as pants and skirts are put on and taken off on a daily basis and need zippers for comfort and convenience. Unless you are planning to change the covers on your pillows with regularity, your pillows do not need zippers. As I mentioned previously, my own pillows do not have zippers and I have never missed them. If, however, you are a confirmed zipper enthusiast, you may want to include them in your designs.

Install a zipper along the bottom edge of a knife-edge pillow, inside the gusset of a box-edge pillow or across the back of either. Be sure to choose a good-quality lightweight zipper that will not add unnecessary bulges to the silhouette of your pillow.

MAKING AND COVERING YOUR OWN PILLOW FORMS

You may want to make and cover your own pillow forms. To do this, follow the directions for the improvised knife-edge pillow on page 26. Make the pillow form out of muslin or other lightweight material. The form should have the same dimensions you want for the finished pillow. Choose a stuffing from those described on page 22.

RUFFLES

Use ribbon, lace or ready-made ruffles to add a soft, feminine look to your pillows. To do this, pin and baste a length of lace or ribbon to the face of one pillow panel around the outside edge. Eyelet lace, available at sewing supply counters, comes already stitched in even ruffles. Fasten a length of this in place, easing it gently around the corners. Ribbon and most types of lace will have to be gathered as you pin. You may be lucky enough to have a ruffle attachment on your sewing machine but, if not, you can create ruffles easily by hand. For full, natural-looking ruffles, you will need a length of ribbon or lace about four times the outside measurement of the pillow. For best results, choose a material that is soft. If the ruffles are to be deep (such as those on the crewel cat pillow on page 53), add additional pins to keep them well away from the seam allowance so they will not be caught in the final stitching. Take a small tuck in the lace or ribbon approximately every ½ inch and pin this tucked lace in position around the pillow panel. The outer, or decorative, edge of the ruffle should be facing toward the center of the pillow. Ease the ruffles around all corners and when the lace has been firmly pinned, baste with small stitches and remove the pins.

Place the pillow back face to face with the pillow front (now including basted ruffle) and proceed with standard pillow construction. The inside edge of the ruffle should be sticking out slightly from between the pillow front and back to insure that it will be caught in the final stitching.

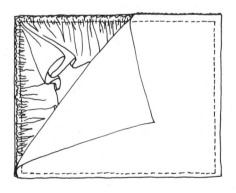

Ruffles

OVERSIZE PILLOWS

Important to any pillow collection are oversize floor pillows. Easy and fun to make at home with simple materials and a sewing machine, giant pillows make great furniture for adults as well as children. Use a portable giant pillow to fill an empty corner or make many oversize pillows to furnish an entire room.

Although giant pillows can be used as sophisticated furniture, there is nothing mysterious about making them (see page 25). For the most part they have the same basic construction as a small two-sided knife-edge pillow. The biggest difference between a 10-inch-square pillow and a 36-inch-square pillow is cost. A standard, small decorative pillow can be made with scraps of material and stuffed with two dollars worth of fiberfill. A large floor pillow will cost considerably more to make. Most people don't have enough large scraps to cover and fill oversize pillows and so they have to purchase what they need.

Fabric for pillow furniture should be strong enough to endure hard wear. Corduroy, velveteen or a good grade of cotton duck, all appropriate, can be expensive in large quantities. Stuffing, too, can be expensive when you are filling a large pillow.

If you are wary of spending money for materials to make pillow furniture, think in relative terms. A large, beautiful Turkish cushion (see page 35) may cost $25 to complete but an equivalent soft, upholstered chair would cost considerably more. In addition, the stuffing (often the biggest investment) is reusable. If the pillow cover itself becomes worn after a few years (whether stained with food or frayed from general wear) you can revitalize the pillow with fresh fabric over the old filling. For more on fillings, see page 21; for more on pillow covers, see pages 25–27.

TURKISH CUSHION

The Turkish cushion, as well as the Turkish bolster (page 141), was inspired by a trip to Fabrications, a dazzling fabric emporium in New York City. Overwhelmed by the striking collection of materials offered by this store, I was particularly captivated by the large, luxurious looking floor cushions covered with warm, hand-printed fabrics. These plump pillows already assembled carried healthy price tags, but Fabrications also sells the makings for them so I decided to buy the fabrics and "do-it-myself" at home.

The fabric I used for the Turkish top was delicately printed with a design inside of a 36-inch square (*plus seam allowance*). The visual effect is similar to a scarf but the Fabrications fabric is considerably stronger. (To make a similar cushion with a scarf, be sure to add a layer of muslin under the scarf for strength.)

The fabric, printed in France, was sold by the square, and after having made so many pillows with scrap material, I found nine dollars for a pillow top exorbitant—and I'm sure the price has gone up since then!

Turkish cushion

On the other hand, the resulting oversize pillow fills a real furniture function. In addition, it has such a special look and feel that this splurge seems to me to have been a justified expenditure. The store also carried French printed fabric with all-over designs to coordinate with the square pillow tops and I couldn't resist buying a half yard, which I later managed to extend into an accompanying bolster (see page 141). I also purchased a yard and a half of heavy duck for a pillow back.

Fabrications sold pillow forms but these I felt I could find elsewhere for less money. Later that week, after some browsing through the classified pages of the phone book, I discovered a neighborhood fabric shop that carried more reasonably priced kapok-filled forms.

Materials Needed:

Finished size: 36 x 36 inches

36 x 36-inch (*plus seam allowance*) printed fabric for pillow front
36 x 36-inch (*plus seam allowance*) cotton duck for pillow back
Sewing machine, needle and thread
Kapok-filled pillow form

To Make This Pillow:

1. Pin printed fabric to cotton duck, *right sides together.*
2. Machine stitch fabric on three sides. Also sew 2 inches in on either side of fourth side of pillow cover. (You will have machine stitched around all four corners—for strength—but left most of the fourth seam open to allow pillow form to be inserted easily.)

Note: If your pillow form has rounded corners you may wish to make Turkish corners for your pillow cover. Refer to page 28 for instructions and make the modification at this point in the pillow construction.

3. Turn pillow cover right side out, insert pillow form and hand stitch cover closed, making sure to fold under raw edges of fabric.

FOUR

Embroidery

Embroidery is the art of decorating fabric with stitchery. Throughout history, embroidery has been a decorating tool of the rich as well as the poor. From opulent patterns on palace draperies to the simplest stitches on crude linen, embroidery has flourished in almost every civilization. Whether the materials are velvet decorated with silk floss or yarn stitched through felt, if the needle and thread have been drawn in and out of the fabric to form decorative stitching on the surface, the process is embroidery.

Embroidery is considered one of the most personal forms of needlework. Learning to embroider is like learning a new alphabet. With a little practice, one has a whole new language to explore. As with the alphabet, everyone works with the same forms, yet each person's work is distinctly different. There are so many variables within the structure of embroidery—from choice of materials to design decisions to the actual placement of stitches—that it can be difficult to duplicate someone else's work without effort.

SUPPLIES FOR EMBROIDERY

Not only is embroidery easy to learn and easy to design, the materials are delightfully inexpensive. You may already have much of what you need in your scrap bag or supply basket, but if not, you'll find it all in your local variety store or five-and-ten. To get started you will need: fabric as a base on which to embroider; yarn or embroidery floss; a long, sharp needle appropriate to the size of the thread; a hoop or frame to keep the fabric taut (this will make it easy to keep your stitches smooth and even); small sharp scissors; and a thimble to protect your finger (optional).

Fabrics

If you are a beginner at embroidery, choose a solid color fabric for your background. Do your first practice stitches on a plain piece of cotton scrap fabric with inexpensive floss. Soon you will be ready to work with more costly materials and threads.

Consider all types of fabric for embroidered pillow stitchery. Any fabric that will not pucker when decorated with stitches is appropriate. In the lightweight category, use muslin or solid color cotton; for medium-weight fabrics, try linen, twill, or kettle cloth. Consider denim, whether bought new or salvaged from a worn-out pair of jeans. For heavy-weight, large pillows use felt, duck, flannel, velvet, velveteen, corduroy or burlap. The medium- and heavy-weight fabrics will be more durable, but the lighter-weight fabrics will accept more delicate stitching.

Check out yard goods shops, department stores and even your scrap basket for materials not readily available in the five-and-ten. Be adventurous. Anything you can push a needle through you can embroider. Once you are experienced you may even want to experiment with embroidery on a patterned background. For more on choosing fabric, see page 13.

Thread

Choose thread according to the weight and texture of the fabric you use. If your background fabric is a delicate cotton or linen, choose an equally lightweight thread. Whatever you plan to use, test the materials together. Make sure the thread will glide easily through the fabric without tearing or pulling (this may be caused by the wrong size needle, too). Also make sure that the thread, floss or yarn is the right weight visually for the thread you have chosen. *Matching the right thread to the right fabric is an important artistic decision.*

When you visit a variety store or craft shop you will be confronted with an infinite selection of threads. The most prevalent (and least expensive) is six-strand embroidery floss, which comes in an inspiring range of colors. This thread can be used as it comes off the skein in the full six strands or the strands can be separated easily for more delicate work. To do this, first cut the floss to a comfortable length (usually 18–20 inches). Separate the strands by rolling the floss between your thumb and forefinger. Gently pull away the extra strands and store them neatly. These extras can be joined later with others and used.

Separating strands of thread

Also consider using better quality threads such as pearl cotton or silk floss. Crochet cotton, string and metallic thread make interesting embroidery. For crewel—a form of embroidery with wool yarn on a coarse background—use tapestry yarn or yarn sold especially for crewel. For special effects, try combining several varieties of thread in one pillow composition.

Needles

Choose a needle according to the fabric and thread you are using. Close-weave fabrics such as linen or denim will require a sharp, pointed needle. Loose-weave cottons like burlap or hardanger will require a needle with a blunt point.

The weight of the thread will also dictate the size of the needle. The eye of the needle should be large enough to accommodate the thread you have chosen but it should not be so big that it leaves a gaping hole in the fabric after each stitch. If the thread falls out of the eye easily, the needle is too big.

Needles are numbered by size. The heavier the needle, the lower the number. The embroidery or crewel needle is long and pointed like a sewing needle but it has a larger eye that can accommodate embroidery floss or crewel yarn. Its sharp point is meant for working on tightly woven fabrics.

The tapestry needle, used for needlepoint, is heavy and blunt. This makes it perfect for stitching into other loosely woven fabric because it slips smoothly through the spaces in the mesh or weave. A chenille needle is similar to the tapestry needle, only it is slightly smaller. It can be used the same way.

Finally, there is the rug needle, which is also similar to the tapestry needle, but larger. Use the rug needle with rug yarn, cord or any other bulky material on loosely woven fabric.

Always use the smallest needle that is comfortable for a job to avoid making unnecessarily large holes in your backing fabric. Keep an assortment of needles in your supply basket so you can choose the right one for each project.

The Embroidery Hoop or Frame

Although you can work on a piece of embroidery while holding it loosely in your hand, you will be disappointed in your stitches if you work this way. Instead, use a hoop or frame to keep your base fabric taut and you will find it easier to keep your stitches even and neat. The hoop, if properly used, will help prevent the fabric from puckering, but you must also be sure not to pull your thread too tightly as you work.

The hoop, available at all sewing supply counters, is made of wood, metal or plastic. Made of two concentric circles that interlock, it usually has a spring or screw arrangement on the outer ring that will allow you to adjust it to the thickness of the fabric. The spring on the metal hoop will adjust automatically, but the wooden and plastic hoops, which must be regulated manually, will last longer. I prefer the wooden hoops and have collected them in lots of different sizes.

To use a hoop, lay the inner ring on a table. Place the fabric to be embroidered on the ring face up, making sure the area of the fabric you're working on is well inside the confines of the circle and is free of folds or creases. Next, place the outer ring over the fabric so it slides snugly over the smaller ring and holds the fabric firmly. Tighten the outer ring if necessary to increase the tension of the fabric. Fabric that is too loose in a hoop will be hard to embroider. Fabric will come loose in a hoop as you work and will need to be tightened at regular intervals. To do this separate the rings, remove the fabric, tighten the outer ring slightly, and begin again. Sometimes the outer ring is too tight to fit safely over the inner ring and fabric. Don't force the fit, you may injure the fabric. Instead, loosen the outer ring and begin again.

Choose a hoop that is smaller than the fabric you are using. For a good grip there should be at least a 2- or 3-inch margin of fabric beyond the hoop on all sides.

Free-standing hoops or clamp-on types can be restricting. In addition, this equipment usually takes up more floor space or table space than the simpler variety.

Still another method of keeping fabric taut while you stitch is to staple or tack the entire fabric to a low cost canvas stretcher used by artists. These are available at art supply stores in any size you need but you must assemble them yourself. Tacks or nails are inexpensive but a staple gun is more efficient. The purchase of a staple gun is costly but it should be considered an investment with many uses.

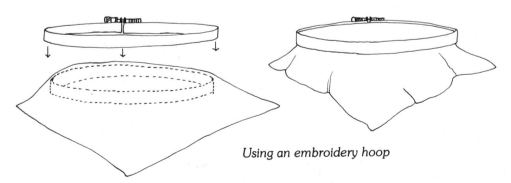

Using an embroidery hoop

EMBROIDERY TECHNIQUES

Designing for Embroidery

Even if you can't draw, you can still design your own needlework. You will get a lot more pleasure from making your own design and you will also save a lot of money.

When you have a copy of your design on paper, including the outside borders of the pillow, you are ready to transfer it to fabric so you can begin to embroider. Choose a fabric that is several inches larger on all sides than the dimensions you have marked for the pillow. If you are cutting fabric from a larger piece, trim it so you have ample seam allowance. It is better to leave too much fabric and trim away the excess when you are ready to do the final pillow construction. On the other hand, don't be afraid to trim your needlework base down to a workable size so you don't have to struggle with an unwieldy piece of fabric. A 3-inch seam allowance on all sides is more than enough.

Before transferring your design to fabric, fold masking tape over the raw edges to prevent unraveling as you work. Or, turn under the edges and hem them loosely.

Once your fabric has been trimmed and hemmed, you are ready to transfer your design to its surface. For this, turn to page 14.

Threading the Needle

Cut your thread to a length just shorter than your arm (usually about 20 inches); any longer and it will tangle and knot as you work, any shorter and you will use it up too quickly.

Threading the needle can be easy once you get the knack. Choose a needle with an eye large enough to hold the thread. Moisten the end of the thread slightly and form it into a point. Stab this into the eye of the needle.

Wool yarn can be trickier to thread until you understand the motion. Some wool yarns are rough in one direction and smooth in the other. Slide the yarn through your fingers to see if you can tell the difference. Thread the needle with the smooth side pointing into the needle because it will slide more easily and there will be less fraying as you work. The stab method recommended for threading floss usually does not work with yarn. Instead, there are two other approaches to use.

To fit heavy yarn into the eye of a tapestry needle you will have to "crimp," or fold, it. Fold the end of the yarn around the eye of the needle and hold it in place with two fingers. With the other hand, pull sharply on the yarn close to the needle to make a crease and flatten the yarn under your fingers. Holding the fold tightly with just a little of the fold extending beyond your fingertips, ease the yarn through the needle's eye. Sometimes it helps to wiggle the folded yarn back and forth until a small amount eases into the needle. As soon as you see that there is yarn in the eye, pull it through the rest of the way with your fingers. If the strands separate during this process and some yarn is left dangling while the rest is in the needle's eye, you will have to remove the yarn and begin again. It's an all-or-nothing process.

The second method for threading yarn through a needle is to use a "flynnder." Using stiff paper, cut a small triangle and fold it lengthwise. Cut a wedge from the corner of an envelope, but be sure to use the fold. Place your yarn in the fold and let the point of the triangle carry the yarn through the eye of the needle. Pull the yarn completely through the eye with your fingers and release the flynnder. This method is especially good for children.

Ending Off

When the thread or yarn gets too short or you want to change colors, end off on the back of the fabric by making a loop with your thread near the fabric and make a knot near the surface of the fabric. If your fabric is very delicate and a knot will cause a bump, end off by making a few running stitches or a backstitch into the stitches that are already in place. It is important to end off while there is enough thread in the needle to create a knot or stitch comfortably. Ending off too soon, except when you are changing colors, can be a waste of thread. With costly silk or metallic threads this can be expensive, but you will soon learn to gauge your timing.

Learning to Stitch

Learning to embroider is like learning to write. Experiment with the stitches that follow on a piece of scrap fabric in an embroidery hoop. With a little practice you will soon be ready to start your first embroidery project.

For practice choose a plain color, medium-weave fabric that is about 8 inches square. Insert the fabric in a hoop. Starting with the first of the stitches described here, try out each stitch one at a time until you have mastered several. Draw lines as you need them with the pencil directly on the fabric to act as stitch guides.

If you allow yourself the luxury of unpressured time, you will be surprised at how easy it is to learn embroidery. It is best not to attach any time limitation to your first experiences. Although I can't predict whether it will take you 10 minutes or 10 days to learn the stitches, be assured that, as with all other new skills, you will improve as you work. As a beginner, don't expect to match those elegant stitches made by your Great-Aunt Agatha, who has been doing embroidery for over 40 years. On the other hand, you should be delighted when you see how a little practice will allow you to make respectable, neat stitches.

STITCHES

The Running Stitch

Try the running stitch first. This is such a simple stitch that even if you are holding a needle and thread for the first time you will do this stitch instinctively.

Draw a straight line with a pencil on the surface to be stitched. Hold the hoop in one hand and with the other hand work the needle. Bring the needle up from the underside of the hoop through one end of the drawn line. You may have to hunt around with the point of the needle until you bring it up in the right place. To do this, poke just the tip of the

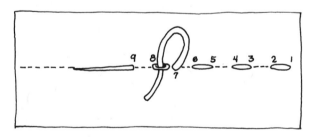

Running stitch

needle through the fabric until you are satisfied with the position; then draw the needle and thread through until just the knot at the end of your thread remains on the back. Always pull gently to make sure the thread is all the way through the fabric, but do not pull firmly enough to cause the fabric to pucker or to pull the knot through the fabric.

Once you have pulled the needle and thread through the fabric you have completed the first part of the stitch. Finish it by poking the needle through the fabric from front to back about ⅛ inch away from where the thread came up, using the drawn line as a guide. What is left on the surface is a short, straight stitch. Repeat, bringing the needle and thread up again about ⅛ inch away from the first stitch along the drawn line. If you are right handed, work from right to left. Lefties will be more comfortable working from left to right. Draw the needle and thread completely through the fabric and tug gently to be sure all the thread has been brought to the surface of the fabric. Do not pull hard enough to cause the fabric to pucker. Thread that has twisted on the underside should be carefully untangled so it too can be drawn to the front. Tangles left on the back of embroidery work will snag future stitches and will cause the kinds of avoidable difficulties that might make you think that embroidery is difficult. Continue stitching along the pencil line until you reach the end of it. End off with a small knot close to the back of the fabric.

Draw another pencil line for practice and start again. It is not necessary to keep your stitches ⅛ inch long, but they should always be sized and spaced evenly. Establish your size and spacing with your first two stitches and then use them as a guide.

When you become comfortable with the running stitch, you will see that it is more efficient to gather several stitches on the needle before pulling the needle completely through the fabric. Learning to gauge the size of your stitches this way can take extra practice, but once perfected, it is a faster method.

If you are working on a curved line, make your stitches smaller and closer together so they follow the curve gracefully.

A large running stitch is called a basting stitch when it is used for temporary fabric tacking. In quiltmaking, a small running stitch is used for quilting several layers of fabric together. When working on embroidery, use the running stitch for outline stitching and straight line details.

The running stitch can be the most versatile of all embroidery stitches. Use it in its simplest form, as described above, or improvise with it by changing colors of thread and stitch direction.

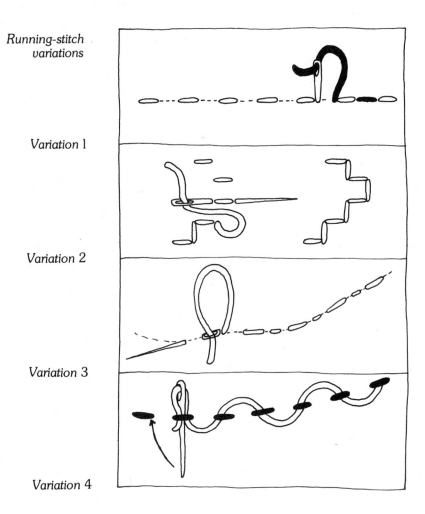

Running-stitch variations

Variation 1

Variation 2

Variation 3

Variation 4

Variation 1
Stitch along a line with one color thread. End off. Stitch back in the other direction using a second color thread to fill in the spaces between the first stitches.

Variation 2
Improvise on the placement of stitches to make geometric borders. If you are using an open-weave fabric such as hardanger cloth (see page 60) or fabric with a regular pattern such as gingham, work all rows in the same direction first and then go back to fill in the spaces in the other direction.

Variation 3
Use long and short running stitches placed close to each other to build surface texture within a shape. Work one row at a time.

Variation 4

Work the running stitch as described along the length of one line and end off. Then, with the same color thread, or one that contrasts, bring the needle and thread up from the back of the fabric to the front under the first running stitch, making sure not to pierce the stitch. Slide the needle and thread under the second stitch and then under the third. Work back and forth so each successive stitch is woven from the opposite direction. If you have trouble preventing the needle from piercing the running stitches, lead with the needle's eye. Control the look of this laced running stitch by the tension of the threading. For a wavy line, keep the lacing loose. For a more refined curve, pull the thread more firmly. End off by bringing the needle and thread to the back of the fabric and forming a knot.

The Backstitch

The backstitch is good for outlines. Going from right to left (for right-hand stitchers), it moves one stitch backward on the surface while moving two stitches forward on the underside of the embroidery.

Draw a line on the surface of your practice fabric. Bring the needle up at point 1, which is just to the left of the beginning of the drawn line. Bring the needle down at point 2, which is where the line actually starts. You have now made your first stitch.

Bring your needle up again at point 3, which is to the left of 1. The distance between 1 and 3 should be the same as the distance between 1 and 2. Continue stitching until the line is complete.

The Stem Stitch

The stem stitch forms a delicate continuous line. Work from left to right, holding the thread below the stitching with the thumb of your left hand as you work. Lefthanded stitchers should work in reverse, from right to left. However, the thread should still be held below the stitching.

Stitch along a drawn pencil line on the surface of your practice fabric. Bring the needle up at point 1, or the beginning of the pencil line. Hold the thread below the line and bring the needle down at 2 and up at 3. Pull gently. Bring your needle down at 4, which is one space to the right, and up again at 5, which is the end of the previous stitch. Continue until you have reached the end of the line. If you are working on a curved line, keep the thread on the outside of the curve. For a finer line, make longer stitches. The crewel cat on page 53 was done almost entirely with stem stitches.

The Buttonhole or Blanket Stitch

This is a good stitch for covering a raw edge of fabric, for stitching down an appliqué shape or for emphasizing an outline in embroidery. It can be worked in a circle to make a sunburst.

The appearance and name of the stitch will vary according to the space and size you choose. Large, open stitches are blanket stitches (originally used to bind blankets). Small, compact stitches are called buttonhole stitches (also used to finish off buttonholes). The appearance will also depend on whether you work on an inside or outside curve.

To start, bring the needle and thread up from the underside and hold the thread below the drawn line on your fabric with your thumb. Bring the needle down through the fabric at 2 and up at 3 (which is below 2). Make sure the thread passes below the needle's point. Gently pull the thread toward you but try to maintain the L shape that the loop will form. Repeat, working from left to right, bringing the needle down at 4 and up at 5. If you are left handed, work from right to left.

Buttonhole or blanket stitch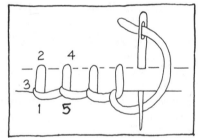

The Chain Stitch

Use this stitch to outline or place them in close rows to fill in a larger area. Work from right to left or top to bottom depending on what is most comfortable for you. At the beginning of the drawn line, bring the needle and thread through at 1. Swing the thread counterclockwise to form a loop. Hold the loop in place with your thumb and put the needle back into point 1. Bring the needle up at 2, making sure the thread is under the needle's point. Pull the thread gently around again toward the left. Repeat the counterclockwise motion to form another loop and insert the needle in 2 (the same hole). Bring the needle up at 3, pull firmly and repeat to form a chain. Stitch until you have completed the line. End off by bringing the needle down over the last loop and end off on the back.

Draw a circle and fill it in with four separated chain stitches to create a daisy (better known as a lazy daisy).

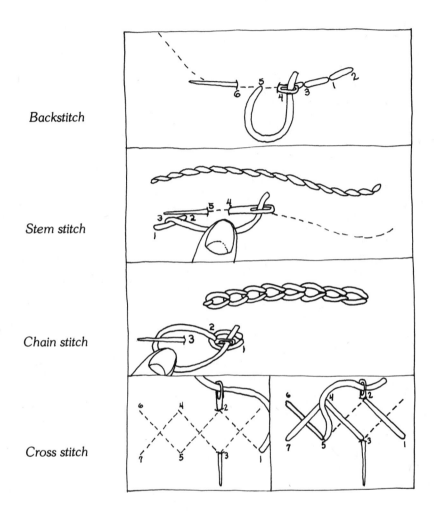

Backstitch

Stem stitch

Chain stitch

Cross stitch

The Cross Stitch

Use this stitch along the edge of a crazy-quilt or appliqué shape. For embroidery, use it in volume to fill in a large shape or use a sprinkling of cross stitches to create delicate texture. Use cross stitch as an unstructured stitch to add to an embroidery design or use it by itself as a counted thread stitch with evenly woven fabrics.

Work this stitch by making a row of slanted stitches from right to left. Complete the row by working back again from left to right, filling in the missing half of the X shapes.

Another method to make cross stitches is by completing one X at a time. To make a row, bring the needle and thread up at 1, down at 2 and up at 3. Tug gently on the thread to make sure it has been drawn through. Bring the needle down again at 4, up at 5 and pull again on the thread. Repeat this process until you reach the end of the line. For neatness, keep all of your stitches as consistent as possible in size, placement and slant. All top stitches should run in the same direction.

For instructions on using the cross stitch as an economical, structured stitch, see illustration, page 64.

The Satin Stitch

The satin stitch is great for filling in areas of embroidery with solid texture. Although the satin stitch is only a series of closely worked straight stitches, it does take practice to gain control. Use it to define direction and shape. Once perfected, it can be one of the most versatile embroidery stitches.

Bring the needle and thread up at 1, down at 2 and up at 3. Bring the needle down again at 4 and up at 5. Continue until you have completely covered an area. After each stitch pull gently on the thread but do not pull too tightly or the fabric will pucker.

Make satin stitches close together, running in a consistent direction. To help keep the outside edging of the stitching even, begin work in the center of a shape and work toward the outer edge. When one side is complete, end off, go back to the center and work toward the other edge.

If an area is extremely large, it is sometimes best to cover it with a pattern of satin stitches. Start in the center of a shape with a slanted satin stitch and fill in one side. Then go back to the center and put in a satin

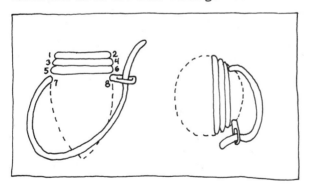

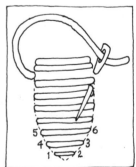

66   Satin stitch   Satin stitch worked from the center   Surface satin stitch

stitch running at an oblique angle. Fill in the second half using this stitch as a direction guide. For added guidance, consider sketching direction lines in pencil on the surface you are embroidering.

To conserve thread, use a surface satin stitch. Bring your needle and thread up at 1, down at 2 and up at 3, as shown. Although this stitch appears to be the same as the regular satin stitch, it is not as strong. The needle and thread do not travel the length of the stitch on the underside of the fabric. Instead they end and begin again on the top of the fabric. The needle catches only a small amount of fabric between stitches.

Variation 1
Use long and short satin stitches for filling in areas and creating shading where a standard one-size stitch would be inadequate. Stagger long and short stitches over the area to be covered.

Variation 2
For a special effect in filling in an area, try gently curving small stitches to delineate a large shape. Add a few direction lines with a pencil inside the design area, as suggested earlier, before you begin to stitch. These markings should help you keep direction shifts smooth and neat.

Variation 3
A simple variation of the satin stitch is the single straight stitch. Use individual stitches to delineate details such as grass, flowers, whiskers or eyelashes.

Special note: The satin stitch should be done with the aid of an embroidery hoop or frame. Without this type of device, the fabric almost always puckers.

Satin-stitch variations

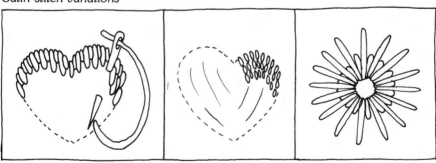

Variation 1:
long and short stitches

Variation 2:
gently curving
small stitches

Variation 3:
individual stitches to
delineate flowers

The French Knot

This stitch is wonderful for flower centers and other areas that benefit from dimension and bulk. French knots make a whimsical texture when clustered together in multiples but they are also effective used singly to highlight other stitches.

Bring the needle and thread up through the spot where the knot is to be. Hold the needle next to the emerging thread and with your free hand, wrap the thread around the needle. Hold the thread firmly and guide the needle into the hole where it emerged. Pull the needle through, leaving a knot on the surface. End off by making a small knot on the back of the fabric. If the needle or the eye of the needle is significantly heavier than the thread you are using you will have trouble making French knots. The hole in the fabric made by the needle will be bigger than the knot itself and the knot will slip through it and fall apart. If you have this problem, choose a smaller needle.

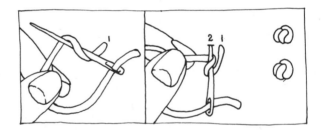

French knot

USING EMBROIDERY TO HIGHLIGHT OTHER PILLOW STITCHERY

Although the pillow projects that follow are straight embroidery, many of the projects in this book contain embroidery as an auxiliary technique. The lace lady (page 163), the yo-yo fish (page 155), and the Liza needlepoint doll (page 86) all contain bits of embroidery. To do these pillows, use the stitch descriptions that have just been given as reference. You will also need embroidery to complete the crazy-quilt pillow on page 190. Consider using embroidery in combination with other techniques in pillow designs of your own.

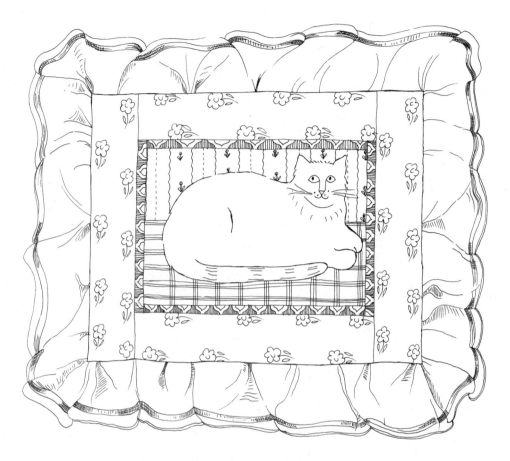

CREWEL CAT

The inspiration for the crewel cat came from a photograph of line embroidery in a French craft magazine. This pillow project turned out to be made entirely from scraps although I spent a lot of time rooting through my materials until I found a combination that seemed right.

Once I decided to do a cat, I measured the fabric available to determine my size and shape limitations. When I decided what dimensions the embroidery base would be, I lined them off on layout paper. By tracing pictures of cats from cat photography books and looking at my own three cats, I began experimenting. After several tries, I came up with a workable drawing.

For the stitching, I used 3-strand Persian wool left over from various needlepoint projects. The full three strands were too bulky for the weight of the linen so I removed one strand from each length that I used. I kept the discarded strands in a neat pile nearby and eventually paired them together and stitched them into the design.

When the embroidery was complete, I began to think about the pillow construction. The embroidered design was only 10 x 7 inches and so a straightforward knife-edge pillow would be very small and insignificant. To avoid this, I decided to make the pillow larger by adding patchwork borders and a ribbon ruffle. The result is a framed fluffy pillow that is really something I'm proud of.

Materials for Needlework:

Finished size: 12 x 15 inches plus 2¾-inch ruffle

Off-white linen or muslin 10 x 7 inches (*plus seam allowance*)
Small skeins of crewel yarn in colors shown in drawing
Embroidery or crewel needle
Embroidery hoop

Materials for Pillow Construction:

Inner patchwork border:
   Two strips of fabric ¾ x 10 inches (*plus seam allowance*)
   Two strips of fabric ¾ x 8½ inches (*plus seam allowance*)
Outer patchwork border:
   Two strips of fabric 11½ x 1¾ inches (*plus seam allowance*)
   Two strips of fabric 12 x 1¾ inches (*plus seam allowance*)
Ribbon or other trim 2¾ inches wide by at least 110 inches long
Fabric for pillow back, 12 x 15 inches (*plus seam allowance*)
Sewing machine (optional)
Pillow stuffing

To Make This Pillow:

1. Scale up drawing on grid to 7 x 10 inches as described on page 16.
2. Trace this onto off-white linen or muslin, leaving a ¼-inch seam allowance on all sides as shown on page 15.
3. Embroider over traced lines, using crewel yarn and needle with stem stitches (as shown on page 49). Follow the colors indicated on the

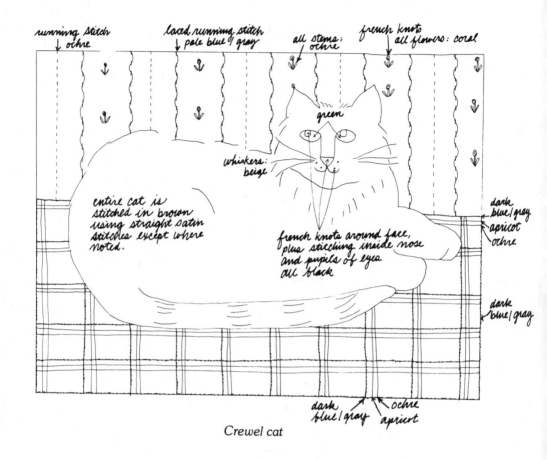

Crewel cat

chart and shown in photograph in color section. Cat's eyes are satin stitch (page 50) and cheeks are French knots (page 52).

4. To do plaid under cat, stitch in blue lines first, then apricot, then ochre, all with stem stitches (see photo for placement).

5. Add patchwork borders next as described in patchwork section on page 119. First add the thin inner border and then the outer border according to the measurements given in the chart.

6. To add ruffle, gather ribbon around the outside edge of embroidered patchwork pillow and pin in position as shown on page 33. Machine stitch in place.

7. Pin completed pillow top face to face with 15 x 12 inch printed cotton backing fabric and complete as described for knife-edge pillow on page 25.

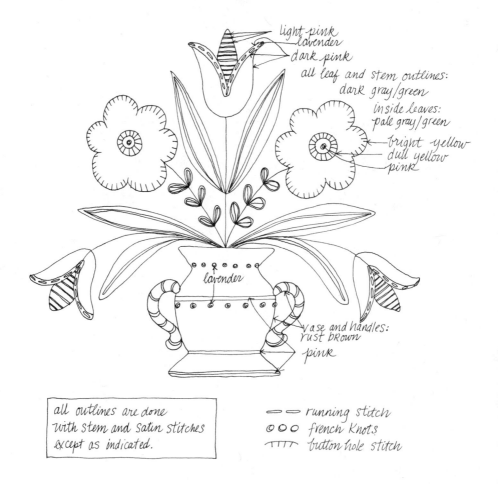

light-pink
lavender
dark pink
all leaf and stem outlines:
dark gray/green
inside leaves:
pale gray/green
bright yellow
dull yellow
pink

lavender

vase and handles:
rust brown
pink

all outlines are done
with stem and satin stitches
except as indicated.

— — running stitch
○ ○ ○ french knots
ᴛᴛᴛᴛ button hole stitch

CREWEL FLOWER BASKET

The crewel flower basket was embroidered and constructed by Vicki Rosenberg with a design and materials that I supplied. Vicki is a wonderful craftsperson and I knew that whatever I designed she would stitch to perfection. For me, this project turned out to be an interesting project in preplanning.

As you probably realize if you have read the description of the crewel cat, I am the sort of needleworker who likes to improvise as I work. Deciding on colors and stitches ahead of time has always been difficult for me. Preparing this project for Vicki forced me to make final decisions right at the start. Yet, when I saw the completed pillow several weeks later, I was delighted.

Even though Vicki had followed my drawing and color scheme, the pillow was not my work. Vicki had followed my instructions and yet managed to make the finished piece distinctly her own. Perhaps this is why mass-produced needlework kits are so popular. No matter what the project, the needleworker always seems to weave something of his or her identity into the finished piece. If you become comfortable designing your own needlework (see page 9), why not assemble a personal needlework kit for a friend. This can be a welcome gift especially if it is for a person like Vicki who prefers to stitch rather than to design.

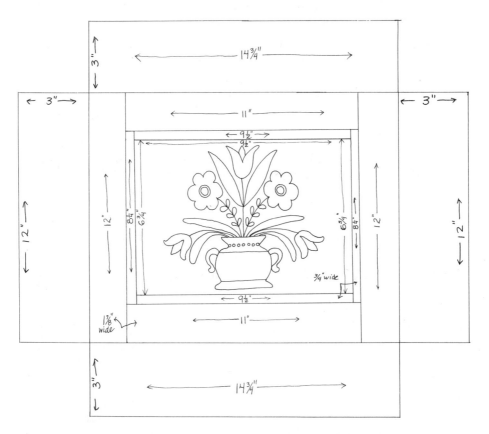

Finished needlework with patchwork borders and 3"-wide boxing.
Add seam allowances to all measurements.

Materials Needed:

Finished size: 12 x 14¾ inches with 3-inch gusset

Off-white muslin or linen 9½ x 6¾ inches (*plus seam allowance*)
Crewel yarn—one small skein of each color shown on chart (or colors of
your choice)
Standard embroidery needle
Two strips of velveteen 9½ x ¾ inches (*plus seam allowance*)
Two strips of velveteen 8¼ x ¾ inches (*plus seam allowance*)
Two strips of gingham 11 x 1⅞ inches (*plus seam allowance*)
Two strips of gingham 12 x 1⅞ inches (*plus seam allowance*)
Two strips of printed cotton 14¾ x 3 inches (*plus seam allowance*)
Two strips of printed cotton 12 x 3 inches (*plus seam allowance*)
12 x 14¾-inch (*plus seam allowance*) piece of same printed cotton for
pillow back
Pillow stuffing

To Make This Pillow:

1. Scale up drawing on grid to 7 inches wide and 6 inches high, as
   shown on page 16.
2. Center and trace this drawing as shown on page 15 onto off-white
   muslin or linen measuring 9½ inches across and 6¾ inches high.
3. Embroider over traced lines using stem stitches. Use French knots for
   the dots, following the chart. Use only 2 strands of the 3-strand crewel
   yarn.
4. Add patchwork border next, beginning with a thin velveteen inner
   border, and then a wider gingham outer border using measurements
   shown in drawing.
5. Add 3-inch-wide printed cotton boxing on all sides as shown on page
   57.
6. Using same printed cotton, add 12 x 14¾-inch pillow back by stitching it face to face with boxing, as shown in instructions for box pillow
   on page 31.

FIVE

Cross Stitch

CROSS-STITCH TECHNIQUES

Cross stitch is the technique of stitching an X shape into a piece of fabric. Although in this century much cross stitchery has been done with the aid of X's stamped or written on fabric, the older, traditional way to create the X shapes is to count the threads in an evenly woven base fabric. By stitching according to the structural mesh of a fabric, the threads of the stitching help strengthen the fabric as opposed to the modern shortcut method in which the stitching just sits on top. Because traditional cross stitching is based on such a clear structure and is so beautiful, this section will deal primarily with cross stitching as a thread-count technique. For those getting started in cross stitching or for those who prefer quicker results, there are two pillows that can be easily stitched on gingham.

Thread-count cross-stitch embroidery has been done in the United States since the beginning of the country itself. Sewing was such a necessary skill in the early years of this country that every girl, rich or poor, was required to learn the basics. Learning to embroider was, for a long time, considered more important than learning to read! Eventually embroidery skills and reading fundamentals were combined in the same lesson—the sampler. Little girls were required to perfect their stitches while depicting the alphabet, numbers, their name and birthdate, as well as a religious thought or quotation. Sometimes names of family members were recorded on samplers.

Although many samplers were purely cross stitch, others were a combination of embroidered stitches. But no matter what else was included, all alphabets and other inscriptions were done with counted-thread stitches. Samplers hanging today in museums, antique shops and private homes are a fascinating source of history of people long forgotten. Usually the stitcher signed her name and age (which tended to be staggeringly young). Samplers were done by young ladies from the age of six and up!

Cross stitch is one of the forms of embroidery that seems to have found a place in the most diverse countries. From Mexico to Rumania, from the Mideast to Scandinavia, cross stitch has been used for centuries as decoration on clothing and home accessories. Thread-count embroidery is such an old technique in Denmark that in 1928 the Danish Design Society was started with the idea of preserving ancient examples of cross stitching and encouraging the interest of modern needleworkers. As part of this plan the society has been publishing, over the years, instruction books on the traditional art of Danish thread-count embroidery. These and other interesting books on thread count or cross stitching can be found in local bookstores and libraries. For specific titles, see page 213.

CHOOSING A PROJECT TO CROSS STITCH

Cross stitching can take on many distinctly different looks and feelings. From my own experience, I have found cross stitching on gingham to be delightfully quick and satisfying. The finished results are very cheerful and tailored. (The flower basket pillow on page 65 was done on gingham.) I have done a few small pieces on hardanger cloth, and the results are much more elegant and formal. But I find handanger much more taxing and hard on my eyes, and for this reason, I suggest that you buy only a small amount of hardanger and pearl cotton if you are trying them for the first time. Or, better yet, try working on gingham first and then graduate to the finer hardanger.

I teach cross stitch to my students at the Fashion Institute of Technology in New York because I feel that it's such an important historical technique. Some students love working on the fine cloths such as hardanger and spend hours creating intricate and exotic counted-thread designs. Others are delighted with the faster possibilities of the more informal gingham and even burlap. Still others have no patience with it at all and would rather be doing less structured embroidery or appliqué. For this reason, I advise newcomers to invest in materials slowly. Hardanger and pearl cotton are too expensive to sit in a drawer half used!

CROSS-STITCH BABY SAMPLER

This cross-stitch sampler was made by Vicki Rosenberg in celebration of the birth of her daughter Sarah. This was a project that I designed and Vicki completed in her own meticulous style. We sent charts back and forth to each other in the mail for several weeks until the sampler with all of its various shapes, borders and letter forms was perfected.

When I sent Vicki the first sampler design, it was based on the alphabets I had seen on samplers from 1775 and 1794, which were missing the letter J. Research turned up nothing and when Vicki wanted to include the J in her sampler, I had no argument. My design, which had been carefully worked out on paper down to the last stitch, now had to be entirely shifted around to include this new addition. The complete alphabet, as stitched by Vicki, is presented here.

Vicki loved doing this project and she has since gone on to do samplers as baby gifts for many of her friends. The finished samplers sometimes take the form of pillows, other times they become wall hangings. She has begun to keep a file of charted motifs such as houses, trees and cats, in addition to the flowers and rabbits in my original design. This is the approach I hope most readers will take to the projects in this book. They are meant as jumping-off points for personal interpretation.

Materials for Needlework:

Finished size: 14 x 14 inches
Sampler: 11 x 11 inches
Gusset: 1½ inches wide

Chart on graph paper with name and birthdate of baby in simple block letters. Use the chart given here as a guide.
11 x 11-inch (*plus seam allowance*) off-white hardanger cloth, raw edges bound with masking tape
Small balls of #8 DMC pearl cotton in colors shown on chart
Embroidery needle
Embroidery hoop

Color guide for
cross-stitch Baby Sampler

☑ light pink
■ dark pink
⊠ light blue
✳ dark blue
☒ light yellow
⊠ dark yellow
⊠ brown
⊠ light green

Cross-stitch baby sampler

For Patchwork Frame:

Two strips of cotton fabric 11 x 1½ inches (*plus seam allowance*)
Two strips of cotton fabric 14 x 1½ inches (*plus seam allowance*)

For Boxing Construction:

Four strips of cotton fabric 14 x 1½ inches (*plus seam allowance*)
14 x 14 inch (*plus seam allowance*) cotton fabric for pillow back
Sewing machine (optional)
Pillow stuffing

Special note: For best results, the fabrics used for patchwork frame, boxing construction and pillow back should all be of the same weight.

To Make This Sampler:

1. Chart your own design on graph paper or follow the chart shown here, changing the name and birthdate to meet your needs.
2. Bind off edges of hardanger cloth with masking tape to prevent raveling.
3. Count horizontal and vertical threads of hardanger cloth to determine horizontal and vertical center and mark these boxes with long basting stitches. This will aid in placement of stitches later.
4. Count and mark central axis of charted design.
5. Begin stitching in the center of design and work outward. Use the cross stitch as shown on page 64. Be sure to stitch over 2 threads at a time.
6. Continue following the chart, working on one small section at a time.
7. When stitching is complete, add 1-inch patchwork border, as shown on page 119, and 1-inch gusset, as shown on page 30. Finish pillow as described for a box pillow on page 30.

CROSS STITCH FLOWER BASKET

The cross-stitch flower basket is a perfect project for a first-time cross stitcher. The materials are inexpensive to buy (some you may already own), the work goes quickly and the results are delightful. The materials are small and light and travel well, making this an ideal lunch break—or even vacation—project. I did this pillow as an improvisation and enjoyed every minute. If you feel adventurous, do the same. Invent as you go along and stitch variations on my arrangements. Or, if you feel more comfortable, follow my chart, which is presented here.

As a base for the cross stitching, I chose pale blue and white gingham with 8 squares to the inch. The fabric was approximately 7½ x 6¾ inches. The design itself was 50 stitches across and 40 stitches high with a 3-square border remaining visible on all sides (plus, of course, the seam allowance). You do not have to use gingham with exactly the same square count per inch as I did but if you follow my chart you will need fabric that contains at least 60 squares across and 50 squares down. Remember, the fewer squares per inch, the larger and more primitive the finished stitchery.

Using graph paper, I planned the flowers, basket and rectangle (representing a tablecloth) for the central motif. When I was satisfied with the shapes, I marked the center axis of the design on paper (by counting squares) and marked the same center lines on the gingham. To mark the paper I used a pencil, but to mark the fabric I used long basting lines (which I removed later).

Although I planned the central motif on paper, the rest of the design I put in mostly by eye. In some cases, the stitches did not fall perfectly in place, which is evident in the decorative border just below the tablecloth area. At first I was horrified at myself for allowing such inconsistency but as work progressed and other motifs were stitched in evenly, I began to notice my early error less and less.

When the cross stitching was complete I added a ½-inch border of smaller-scale gingham (10 squares to the inch) and a 1½-inch border of cotton fabric with a small geometric print. If your design is stitched on a different-size gingham, you will have to adjust the size of your borders by eye. A smaller design should have a more delicate border and a larger design a more robust one. The finished pillow is a knife-edge and the backing is the same geometric print as the outer border of the pillow face.

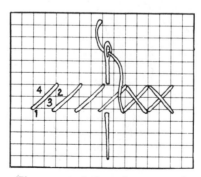

The counted-thread cross stitch

Materials Needed:

Finished size: 10¾ x 11½ inches
Cross-stitch panel: 6¾ x 7½ inches plus patchwork borders

6¾ x 7½-inch (*plus seam allowances*) gingham with 8 squares to the
  inch, or gingham in measurements appropriate to your design
Small skeins of embroidery floss in colors shown on chart
Embroidery needle and hoop
For inner border:
  Two strips of cotton fabric 7½ x ½ inches (*plus seam allowances*)
  Two strips of cotton fabric 7¾ x ½ inches (*plus seam allowances*)
For outer border:
  Two strips of cotton fabric 1½ x 8½ inches (*plus seam allowances*)
  Two strips of cotton fabric 1½ x 10¾ inches (*plus seam allowances*)
11½ x 10¾-inch (*plus seam allowance*) cotton fabric for pillow back
Sewing machine (optional)
Pillow stuffing

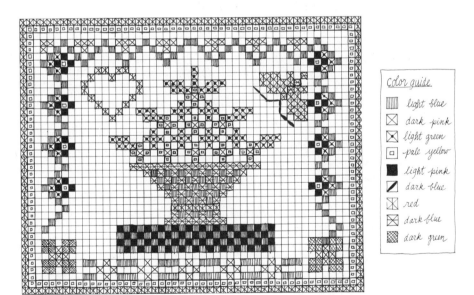

Cross-stitch flower basket

To Make This Pillow:

1. Chart your own flower basket or use the chart shown here.
2. Cut gingham with 8 squares to the inch to 7½ x 6¾ inches (*plus seam allowance*) on all sides.
3. Put a basting line down the horizontal and vertical center of fabric with long basting stitches and mark these same centers on graph chart with darkened line. To find centers, count the boxes and divide in half.
4. Starting from the center of the chart, stitch in design on fabric, putting 1 cross stitch in each box, as shown.
5. When cross stitch is complete, add patchwork borders as described on page 119, following the dimensions given in materials section or appropriate to your design.
6. Construct the pillow in the knife-edge style (page 25) using printed cotton fabric measuring 11½ x 10¾ inches or appropriate size (*plus seam allowances*) for pillow back.

CROSS-STITCH PILLOW FOR MOLLY

I made the cross-stitch pillow as a gift for newborn Molly Mandel. After working with slow, painstaking cross stitch on hardanger cloth for some other projects, stitching on gingham came as a welcome change. For Molly's pillow I chose large 4-square-to-the-inch blue and white gingham. I wanted to do special needlework as a baby gift but I wanted the finished piece to be sturdy enough for the baby to be able to play with. The pillow for Molly came together with a minimum of fuss and I enjoyed every moment. It is a project I would recommend for any needleworker looking for a personalized baby gift idea.

I worked from the center outwards, completing the cross-stitched nameplate and then going on to the actual pillow construction. Using graph paper and a pencil, I charted out Molly's name plus a simple border decoration. I counted the boxes in the graph paper design including the extra rows around the outside of the border stitching and lined off the exact area on the wrong side of the gingham, using a pencil and ruler. I needed to have these boundaries visible on the right side as well, so I used a long basting stitch to trace over the drawn line. This line was visible while I did my embroidery and was easy to remove when the stitching was complete. The dimensions of the central panel are 7¼ x 3½ inches (or 4 squares by 24 squares) but unless you are making a pillow for a little girl named Molly, your dimensions are bound to be different. To do a pillow with any other name, the best approach is to plan the center panel on graph paper first, as I did, and let the size of this dictate your other dimensions.

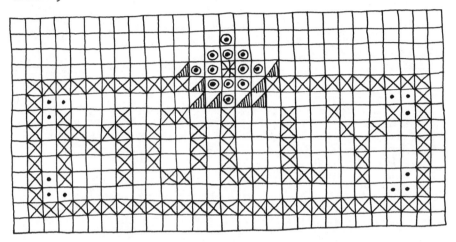

⊠ Outer border: yellow
   Name: red

▣ blue
▣ gold

◩ green
   red

Pillow Construction: Sham Style

When the pillow top was complete, I placed it face to face with the back fabric, which matched it in size (including the seam allowance) and stitched them using a machine straight stitch, leaving about 3 inches open on one side for the stuffing. I trimmed the corners and turned the pillow right side out.

If this had been a standard knife-edge pillow I would have then added stuffing. Instead, this was to be a pillow-sham construction so there were a few more steps.

I smoothed the pillow flat with the side of my hand and put in pins at right angles to the seam that joined the two border fabrics to hold them in place. With the sewing machine, I ran a straight stitch in this seam almost completely around the perimeter of the pillow, sewing the pillow front to the pillow back. I left a 13-inch opening in this stitching parallel to the opening on the outside edge.

Using a crochet hook, I pushed Dacron fiberfill through these two openings into the central area of the pillow. The cross-stitched panel and red border fabric would be stuffed as part of the pillow. The yellow border was to remain flat as part of the decorative edge. I added stuffing until the pillow was gently full, being careful to make sure it reached the corners. Too much filling would have caused the inner stitching to buckle; too little and the pillow would have looked like a pancake. When I was satisfied with the amount and the placement, I closed up the inner stitching with the sewing machine. The outer edge I turned in and stitched closed by hand.

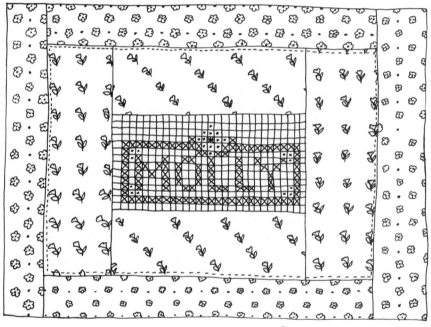

Cross-stitch pillow for Molly

Materials Needed:

Finished size: 14½ x 11½ inches
Cross-stitch panel: 7 x 3½ inches

Chart on graph paper with name of child in simple block letters. Use example shown here, as well as sampler also shown in this section, as a guide.

Cotton gingham with 4 squares to the inch, 7 x 3½ inches (*plus seam allowance*) or size that is appropriate to the name you are using

Two small skeins of 6-strand embroidery floss in each color shown on chart

Embroidery needle and hoop

Four strips of cotton fabric for inner border in dimensions appropriate to your design. Width of inner border strips should be approximately 2¾ inches.

Four strips of cotton fabric for outer border in dimensions appropriate to your design. Width of outer border should be approximately ¾ inch.

Cotton fabric for pillow back in dimensions that are the same as completed pillow front (name panel plus patchwork strips—*remember to allow for seams*)

Sewing machine (optional)

Pillow stuffing

To Make This Pillow:

1. Using simple block letters, chart name on graph paper.
2. Cut gingham 7 x 3½ inches (or size that is appropriate to your design) *plus seam allowance* on all sides.
3. Put a basting line down horizontal center and vertical center of gingham. To find the centers, count the boxes and divide in half. Mark the same centers on graphed chart with darkened line.
4. Starting from the center of chart, stitch in design on fabric, putting 1 cross stitch in each box as shown.
5. When cross stitching is complete, add patchwork borders as described on page 119, using dimensions that are appropriate to your design.
6. Construct the pillow in the pillow-sham style as described on page 67, using a backing fabric in the same measurements as the completed cross stitch.

SIX

Needlepoint

NEEDLEPOINT TECHNIQUES

Needlepoint is the technique of stitching yarn into a mesh until the entire surface is covered. Of all the hand embroideries, needlepoint is the strongest and longest lasting. You may have trouble thinking of needlepoint as embroidery, but consider that crewel embroidery, silk and cotton embroidery and cross-stitch embroidery are all worked into a backing fabric that is usually of linen, cotton or wool. Needlepoint, too, is worked into a backing fabric. The major difference is that with embroidery, the cotton or wool background is left blank in many areas and these blank spaces act as part of the needlework design. The stitches sit on top of the fabric. With needlepoint, the entire backing must be covered or interwoven with strands of yarn. This gives the completed stitchery a special kind of strength and durability. Try removing some stitches from a crewel embroidery. They usually come free with a few snips of the scissors and a pull of the needle. Now try removing the same amount of stitching from a needlepoint canvas. It takes time and patience to free the strands that have been tightly woven into the needlepoint mesh. Because of this strength, a needlepoint project usually takes more time to complete than other kinds of embroidery. However, the resulting needlepoint "fabric" will outlive the cotton- or wool-backed embroidery composition.

Aside from strength, needlepoint stitchery is beautiful to look at and fun to do. It is so easy to learn that it can accommodate the uncertain beginner, but because there is so much room for experimentation, it is also ideal for the fearless expert. There are endless possibilities within the framework of the mesh, allowing the needlepointer to work up a design using one basic stitch or to experiment with a variety of textural stitches.

Every needleworker has her or his favorite stitchery. Needlepoint is mine. Although I also enjoy other forms of stitchery, I like needlepoint for its rich wool colors, textures and the structure of its canvas backing. I get tremendous satisfaction from choosing colors from the variety of soft Persian wools that are available. I love to design on paper for needlepoint, transfer the drawing to canvas and then, finally, paint with the yarn. Needlepoint stitching is slow but when I hold a completed piece of needlepoint in front of me, I know I have created a new, durable fabric. For years, I have been designing simple shapes for needlepoint, tracing them onto mesh with a waterproof marker and then stitching. Lately I have begun to enjoy working on a blank canvas without a predetermined design. By lining out a basic shape on the canvas and then marking off any large areas within that, I have filled in the areas with innumerable textural stitches and colors. I enjoy the flexibility and (admittedly) the surprise of this method. If you are an experienced needleworker and would like to try working with improvisation as I have done, see page 77 for more information. If you are a novice at needlepoint, read on.

Materials for needlepoint

BUYING MATERIALS

The impulse of most people beginning a craft for the first time is to buy a kit. With needlepoint, especially, this is a *bad* idea. Most inexpensive needlepoint kits geared for the beginner teach bad stitch habits by advocating the use of half cross stitch. This stitch uses less yarn than the continental or (my favorite) basketweave stitch, and therefore costs the manufacturer less to package. But the half cross stitch barely covers the canvas, wears badly and takes as much time to do as the continental or basketweave. Except for the very expensive ones, needlepoint kits are generally filled with poor quality materials. You will do much better if you visit a needlework specialty shop and purchase small amounts of good quality supplies. Also inexpensive materials are often hard to handle. This can be unnecessarily discouraging. Inexpensive canvas is coarse and it can be difficult to pull the yarn through it smoothly. The constant tugging may weaken or even break the yarn. If you are trying needlepoint for the first time, approach it with respect—for both the materials and yourself as a craftsperson. Don't skimp on quality.

What to Buy

Next, take a trip to the shop of your choice and purchase a small amount of 10-thread-to-the-inch mono canvas for needlepoint. All you will need is ¼ to ½ yard. Also choose several ounces of Persian wool in colors that appeal to you, a blunt tapestry needle with a large eye and a waterproof felt marker (usually carried by these shops). If you don't have a needlepoint shop locally (don't forget to try department stores) check the listing on page 212 for mail-order addresses.

Buy 1-inch masking tape to bind the rough edges so your yarn will not get caught as you work and so the mesh does not unravel.

You will also need small, sharp scissors.

Beginning to Work

Cut a 2 x 2 inch square of mesh and fold masking tape over the raw edges. With your marker, line off an approximately 1-inch square, tracing along on the lines of the mesh.

To begin, there are two basic stitches to know. On the front surface of the mesh they appear to be exactly the same but they are actually quite different in structure.

Thread a single piece of yarn (which is made of three twisted strands) through the needle by flattening it with your thumb and forefinger and easing it through the needle's eye. Knot the end. This knot is only made for the first stitch on the mesh. All other new lengths are woven into the existing stitches.

THE CONTINENTAL STITCH

This stitch is worked from right to left in straight lines. When you have reached the end of one row, simply turn the canvas upside down and work in the other direction.

To make your first stitch, think of the needle placement in terms of four quadrants that are formed when two strands of the mesh cross. When beginning the continental stitch always bring the needle from the back of the canvas to the front through the lower left quadrant. To complete the stitch, bring the needle down again, through the mesh to the back through the upper right quadrant. The stitch, when done correctly, sits on a diagonal. To make the next stitch, bring the needle up again immediately to the left of the stitch you have completed. You will be delighted to see that the wool is in the correct position for you to repeat the same sequence and create the second stitch. Continue stitching until you have completed a row of 7 or 8 stitches (or have reached the drawn boundaries). After each stitch, pull your yarn gently against the mesh. Don't pull too tightly because this will eventually distort the mesh and put too much pressure on the yarn.

When you have reached the end of one row, simply turn the canvas upside down and work in the other direction as shown below in steps 3 and 4. You will always be working with the front of the canvas, the side with the pattern marked on it, facing you.

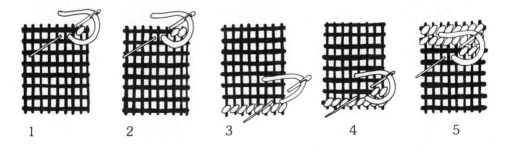

1   2   3   4   5

The continental stitch may seem easy and repetitous and, in fact, it is. But learning to stitch with even tension and placement of color is the key and can take experience. Now that you see how simple this basic stitch is, you should have no fear about learning the more subtle refinements.

THE BASKETWEAVE STITCH

The basketweave appears on the surface to look exactly like the continental stitch but in structure it is quite different. It gets its name from the pattern that the yarn makes on the back of the mesh, which is woven like a basket. The pattern on the back of continental stitching is even, vertical rows formed by the needle working from right to left.

The basketweave is worked on the diagonal in ascending and descending rows. Learning to place these stitches in the right sequence is a little more challenging than learning the continental stitch, but the basketweave (also known as the diagonal stitch) is worth the extra effort. The basketweave uses more yarn in its woven structure and therefore covers the mesh completely. The continental stitch tends to pull the canvas into a lopsided posture. This disfigurement, which is unavoidable, can only be corrected in blocking the finished piece. Sometimes this blocking takes four or five tries. The basketweave, on the other hand, distributes the tension of the stitching more evenly and creates less canvas distortion. The finished piece is easier to block.

The continental stitch is good for tight places or doing straight line detail. The basketweave is especially good for backgrounds and all other areas that are large enough to establish a routine.

If you have learned needlepoint from a commercial kit, you are probably already hooked on the continental or even the half cross stitch recommended by manufacturers. Learn to use basketweave for your

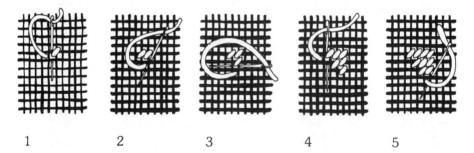

1   2   3   4   5

own designs and your needlepoint will look better and wear longer. Of course, don't try using basketweave with a kit unless it is recommended. You won't have enough yarn!

Start the basketweave in the upper right-hand corner of the canvas. If you are careful to alternate your ascending and descending rows, your stitches will always mesh smoothly. Some jumping around with your stitches is sometimes unavoidable. Two rows running in the same direction will cause a slight raise so if you are working on a background area, try to keep track of your directions.

Prepare another 2 x 2 inch square as you did to learn the continental stitch, complete with lined off 1-inch box and taped edges.

Thread the tapestry needle with a strand of Persian wool and knot the end.

Starting in the upper right-hand corner of the mesh, bring the needle from the back of the canvas to the front as you would for the continental stitch. Bring the needle down again through the upper right diagonal hole, as shown.

Row 2 is a descending row. Made this stitch immediately to the left of stitch 1. So far this stitch is very similar to the continental!

The second stitch in row 2 is made immediately below stitch 1, as shown. Bring the needle diagonally across the mesh from lower left to upper right.

Row 3 is ascending. Make the first stitch in row 3 immediately below the last stitch in row 2, as shown. The second stitch in row 3 falls into the open gap between the two stitches in the second row. The third stitch is made immediately to the left of the first stitch in row 2.

Take a look at your stitching if you have successfully completed the first three rows so far to see what this seemingly complicated arrangement of stitches is really doing. If your mesh is a tangle of yarn and misplaced stitching, carefully cut the yarn away, look at the diagram shown here and get ready to try again. You are setting up an arrangement of interlinking stitches but at the same time you are beginning and ending rows and defining the top and right side of a square as you work. Learning this initial setup is the hardest part of learning basketweave. As the rows get longer, the stitching becomes easier to understand.

Row 4 is descending. Follow along on the diagram if, for the moment, you have given up stitching. Stitch 1 is made immediately to the left of the last stitch in row 3. Stitch 2 is made in the space between the last 2 stitches in row 3. Stitch 3 is made in the space between stitch 1 and 2 of row 3. Stitch 4 is made just below the first stitch in row 3.

Now that you have followed the chart and possibly fumbled through your first experience with basketweave, you are probably thoroughly confused. I know I was the first few times I tried it. If you can understand the theory of the stitch placement, you will see that it is a very logical stitch. Because needlepoint is worked on a rigid mesh of squares, each diagonal row that you stitch properly is composed of staggered stitches—one in, one out, one in, one out—until the row is completed. Each space that you leave by stitching a descending row will be neatly filled in when you return with an ascending row. If you find yourself making stitches exactly next to each other, you are doing something wrong. With the exception of the first and last stitch in each row, basketweave stitches should always fit snuggly into a gap between two stitches in the row before. At the same time, they are setting up gaps of their own.

Having been through your first attempt at basketweave with or without success and having now read this new information, go back to the beginning and try again. If you are still confused, look carefully at the chart until you can see that each row is made of staggered stitches and each new row is constructed in the gaps between the stitches of the previous row. If you can get beyond the first four rows, the rest is easy. It's worth the few minutes of struggle because once you do figure it out, you will have it forever. There will be no stopping you!

Changing Yarn

When the yarn in your needle gets down to the last few inches or it's time to change color, end off by pulling the needle and yarn under 3 or 4 stitches on the back of the canvas so it is well woven. Snip off the remaining yarn with scissors close to the mesh but be careful not to cut into anything but the intended strand.

To start a new piece, thread the needle but do not knot the yarn. Instead, run the yarn through the stitching already in place on the back near where you intend to resume your stitching. Make sure it is firmly anchored and then draw it through the mesh in the correct place.

Length of Yarn

A good length to choose if you have to cut your yarn for needlepoint is approximately the length of your arm. Too long and it will be unwieldy. Too short and you will be slowed down by changing strands too often.

When stitching your rows, work your yarn as short as possible but plan to end off with enough left for you to comfortably weave the needle in and out of the existing stitches.

DESIGNING FOR NEEDLEPOINT

There are three basic approaches to designing for needlepoint and each approach suits a different need.

The first approach is to use a simple drawing. Trace it onto the needlepoint mesh with a waterproof marker and then fill in the areas with appropriate colors.

The second method is to chart out each stitch on graph paper (as for cross stitch) and then copy each mark onto the canvas by eye. If you like doing cross stitch you will like this too. If you intend to create a well-integrated pattern, use method one. The chart method is good for designs such as traditional American samplers or geometric folk patterns from other countries. Craft magazines often give charted directions for duplicating a needlepoint project because the chart allows them to account for every stitch. Working from a chart can be very challenging and I know people who thrive on it. I, for one, prefer the freedom of working with a simple drawing or with the method of improvisation, which follows.

Improvising, the third method, is for the adventurous. Mark out a basic outline on your needlepoint canvas. Use the stitches suggested here or any other stitch guide, a basketful of yarn, and experiment. Most decorative needlepoint stitches can be learned with just a little practice. Play with these stitches to create an infinite variety of textures. Dorothy Globus's circular pillow on page 95 as well as my patchwork and tree pillows on pages 99 and 89 were created this way. For more on this approach, turn to page 99 (the patchwork pillow).

Preparing the Canvas

When preparing the canvas, whatever design method you choose, fold masking tape over the raw edges of the canvas to prevent it from unraveling and snagging the yarn. Don't turn the edges under and sew them because this will still leave rough edges to catch the yarn. Instead, if you want to sew, stitch on binding tape to seal off the ragged edges.

When planning a design, always leave at least three rows of mesh, if not more, for blocking room and seam allowance around the outside edge of the design.

Design Sources

When it comes to designing for needlepoint, or any other technique in this book, there are countless sources to consult. The trick is to choose designs appropriate to the capabilities of the technique you are using. Needlepoint is done on a square framework; therefore, it is impossible to make perfect curves. This does not mean that you should plan to do only straight lines. Instead, plan large, loosely flowing designs. Allow for the built-in geometry of the needlepoint mesh. If you must have accurate circles, consider appliqué, embroidery or stencil.

Turn to the countless wonderful craft books and magazines for picture reference and ideas. Don't be afraid to trace anything that you see for use in your needlepoint, but trace first onto paper rather than onto your mesh. This intermediate tracing will give you the opportunity to make changes. Make any adjustments that seem right. This can only help to make your needlework more personal.

Drawings in books and magazines often have to be enlarged before use. For specifics on how to do this, see page 16. For more on creating your own needlework designs, be sure to turn to page 9.

One of the wonderful things about needlepoint is the ease with which you can become experienced, or even expert. Because the tools are so manageable, all you really need is some good reference material and the desire to experiment. Thousands of people in this country are already enjoying the pleasures of needlepoint. The question is, how many have become independent enough to design their own?

Transferring a Design to Canvas

Once you are satisfied with your design on paper, it's time to transfer it to the needlepoint canvas. Go over the outline again with a soft pencil or marker to darken all the lines. When this is done, tape the paper design to a table top or other hard surface. Tape the canvas in position over this design so the design is well centered. It is a good idea to have your masking tape binding in place around the rough edges of the canvas before you begin work with the mesh. Without it, you will see how quickly the mesh begins to fray.

Trace the design including the outside borders from the paper onto the canvas mesh, using a waterproof felt-tipped marker or acrylic paint and brush. It is absolutely necessary that what you use be completely waterproof. This is because you will have to wet your completed needlepoint to block it back into shape. Imagine the frustration if, after all those hours of work, your efforts are ruined by running ink! Needlework shops, hardware stores and art supply stores sell markers of all different brands. To test the markers, try writing with one on a piece of paper, let it dry *completely* and then drip water on it. If the color smears at all, avoid the marker. Ask to try another type until you find one that does not smear.

Be wary of prepackaged markers designated for needlework. Test these as you would any other. Nothing is above suspicion. Sad to say, I have learned the hard way with a package of felt-tipped pens that promised that they were for use on needlepoint. But I was lucky. The color ran only around the outside edge of the stitching, so that, by making the pillow top slightly smaller than planned, I could salvage my needlepoint.

If you prefer to use paint to delineate your design, use acrylic paint only. The tube should be marked *waterproof,* rather than water-resistant. Acrylics are available at art supply stores in a huge range of colors. For easy handling, they may be thinned with water or polymer medium, available where the paints are sold. Neither water nor polymer will change the nature of the acrylic. It dries into a tough plastic, so be sure to wash out your brush or wipe up any unwanted spots with mild soapy water while they are still wet.

Do not under any circumstances use watercolors or gouache on your canvas. They will bleed when moistened. Do not use oil color. It takes many days to dry and then never dries thoroughly.

To Color or Not to Color Your Canvas

Once you have traced your outline onto canvas with a dark line, you may want to color in each area. This is the way commercially prepared canvases are sold and if you are a beginner you may find this helpful. To me, as an experienced needlepointer, the addition of color is confusing and often confining. The colors of the acrylic paint rarely match the intended colors of wool. Although large areas of color can help guide you as you stitch, for the most part the painted picture interferes with making color decisions. I prefer to trace the design on canvas with a black line and then stitch into the natural canvas. I can see immediately how the colors of wool interact with each other without the interference of the painted color. I do occasionally color in the original design on paper to try out color ideas. I keep this sketch nearby as I work for reference. Since this color is only on paper and it will not touch the needlepoint canvas, I am not bound to using waterproof markers. I can use anything that's handy such as pastels, colored pencils or crayons.

Reading a Stitch Chart

In the needlepoint stitch charts in this book, a single diagonal mark shown within a box indicates a continental or basketweave stitch. A letter or symbol shown within a box indicates a continental or basketweave stitch in the color shown in the accompanying legend. Longer marks indicate direction and length of straight bargello stitching (made like embroidered satin stitching) in which yarn is drawn over several threads of embroidered mesh.

Buying Materials for Your First Project

Once you have your design on paper you are ready to buy wool. Take your design to a local needlework shop to help you choose amounts. A swatch of fabric, a snip of wallpaper or another pillow from the area where the pillow will be used can be just what you need for color direction. If this isn't possible, choose crayons or colored pencils that blend with the area and color in your design before you go to buy yarn. If you are working without a place for the finished pillow in mind, choose a scarf, a china cup or even a picture with colors that you enjoy.

Knowing how much yarn to buy comes with experience. For your first purchase, ask for help from the salesperson. This person will not be able to tell exactly how much you need because everyone works differently but she or he will be able to set you in the right direction. It is far better to buy more yarn than you need than less. Good quality Persian yarn stores well, and leftovers from one project can be the inspiration for another. Also, it may be difficult to purchase small amounts of yarn later to finish off a project. Some shops will sell single strands in case you run short at the end of your stitching but this can be expensive as well as inconvenient. Be sure to indicate to the salesperson which stitch you intend to use and (if you aren't buying canvas at that time) what size mesh. Basketweave uses about one-third more wool than continental. The smaller meshes (12 and 14 squares to the inch) eat up wool faster than mesh that is 10 to the inch. For a first needlepoint it's best to start with 10-thread-to-the-inch mesh, but once you have completed your first needlepoint project you may want to experiment with other sizes and types. When you are ready for this, again rely on the salesperson for advice and direction. Some of the more advanced needlepoint projects in this collection were done on these smaller meshes. Specific information on how to use these canvases is given in each section.

BLOCKING NEEDLEPOINT

Blocking needlepoint, or pulling it back into shape once the stitching has been completed, is a procedure that many needlepointers would rather leave to the experts. I was once one of these people—afraid to see my needlepoint through to the finished pillow. Then I met Joan, an avid needlepointer who had actually blocked and sewn all of her own pillows. When I expressed my amazement at her bravery and skill, she only laughed. Needlepoint, she told me, was her first love and only accomplishment. She claimed to have never sewn a hem or darned a sock. She did not find needlepoint difficult, in fact, she found it relaxingly easy. When she was ready to have her first two or three creations converted into pillows, she found the cost prohibitive. Rather than leave her pillow tops unused in a drawer, she decided to do the conversion herself. A little research in the library, a pencil and ruler, borrowed hammer and tacks, an ancient sewing machine (which she had never used) inherited from an aunt, and she was ready to go. Her description of the process made it seem easy, especially when she assured me that she had no secret skills. She had learned just enough sewing to complete a pillow top. Her machine was so primitive that it would only straight stitch forward.

Joan's enthusiasm and finished pillows left a big impression. Certainly if she could make needlepoint pillows with no previous experience, using the most primitive equipment, I could master the technique with my staple gun and slightly more up-to-date sewing machine.

Armed with a few library books, but making no secret of my fear that I might inadvertently destroy the piece of needlepoint that I had so lovingly and painstakingly stitched, I began to block my first pillow. What I soon discovered was that blocking is a straightforward, basically simple procedure. It does take a few minutes of determined pulling, stretching and stapling. A hammer and upholstery tacks would do the job as well. I learned, also, that the blocking process sometimes has to be repeated two or three times, until a piece of needlepoint is coaxed back into the correct shape. By far the most difficult part of learning the whole technique was waiting for the needlepoint to dry thoroughly so I could remove it and admire the finished work! It was exhilarating to realize that blocking was not the great mystery I had thought it to be. I am delighted to report that it is a skill easy enough to be learned by anyone with the perseverance to complete a needlepoint. For those of us on budgets, it is a great relief to know that here is one more technique that can be done successfully at home without the help of a high-priced craftsperson. In addition, once the blocking has been completed (don't forget it can take several tries depending on how misshapen your needlepoint has become during stitching), pillow construction takes only a few more minutes.

Materials Needed for Blocking Needlepoint

Large, clean wooden board (if possible with straight edges)

Special note: I have an old wooden worktable that I use. I tape clean brown paper to it and staple directly into this. My friend Joan uses the wooden floor in her bedroom (but don't tell anyone you read that here).

Sheet of clean brown wrapping paper that has been taped to the wooden surface

Staple gun. A hammer and tacks can also be used but I find them hard to handle. Before investing in a staple gun, try borrowing one.

Special note: Whichever you use, staples or tacks, make sure they are rustproof by soaking them in water for an hour first.

Metal T-square or right angle. The person who lends you the staple gun will probably also have one of these tools too. Otherwise, invest in one from the hardware or art supply store. This is a tool you will find invaluable.

How to Block Needlepoint

Wet the back of the needlepoint with a clean, wet sponge or hold the needlepoint under a gently running tap of warm water. Don't let the water soak in completely, but move the needlework around so the back is slightly moistened. This will happen in just a few seconds if you tilt the piece and allow the water to run off the sides. Give the needlepoint a slight shake to remove any excess water. If you use the sponge method, keep a bowl of clean water nearby. Dip the sponge in water, wring it out and then dab on the back of the needlepoint. Repeat this until the entire back is wet.

At this moment you may have panicked. Dampening the needlepoint has dissolved the sizing that had been stiffening the mesh. Instead of holding a needlepoint, you feel like you are holding a wet noodle. Fear not, once the piece has dried thoroughly, it will stiffen up again. But now, while it's soft and pliable, is the time to pull it into shape.

With the needlepoint lying face down in the center of the board covered with paper, put some staples into the needlepoint mesh with about a row of mesh between the staples and the edge of the stitching. There are two theories on the placement of staples (or tacks) for blocking. Consider both of them and decide which you like best. Theory one is that staples should be placed along an entire side, then the facing side, then a third side and finally, the fourth side. The last 6 inches of the fourth side will require extra tugging against the sides already stapled to pull it square.

Theory two is that single staples are first applied in the center of each side. Progressive staples are placed in alternating sides working from these center staples out toward the corners.

I usually combine the two methods by putting 2 or 3 staples in the center of each side, alternately. The tricky part is to make sure you have pulled as firmly as possible on the canvas at the same moment you have inserted the staple or tack, making the canvas as taut as a drum. Don't let the wet noodle effect fool you. The canvas and needlepoint are stronger than you are. In fact, it's doubtful that you are strong enough to pull the needlepoint square on the first blocking.

The only real problems that might arise are that you did not leave enough extra mesh around the edge of your needlepoint so you can't get a good grip or that the masking tape begins to pull away from the mesh. In either case, grasp the needlepoint instead of the mesh and staple closer to the stitching. In extreme cases, you may have to staple into the stitching itself, so make extra sure the staples or tacks are rustproof. If the masking tape has pulled away, continue to pull and staple, but be gentler. When the canvas has dried completely, remove the staples or tacks, retape the injured edges and begin again. The first blocking will make the second go-round much easier.

Squaring

Use an accurate T-square, right angle or drafting triangle to measure the sides and corners as you work. Often two sides and part of a third will appear to be perfectly straight and squared off, while the remaining side and a half and one corner are still off kilter. Remove the staples from the offending areas and pull again until you have coaxed these areas into a closer approximation of what they should be. There is a wedge on the staple gun that will make this easier. To remove tacks, a blunt kitchen knife works well.

Most pieces, depending on your style of stitching and the stitches you have used, require two or three blockings to get them square. Each successive attempt becomes easier. Needlepoint done with a lot of continental stitching may take four or more blockings, depending on how tight you've made your stitches.

Don't be intimidated by this prediction; after all, each blocking only takes about fifteen minutes of work. Even two hours of work time spent blocking is nothing compared to the time spent doing the actual stitching. The rest of the time is taken up by drying.

Drying Time

Drying time may take anywhere from overnight in a steam-heated apartment to a few days in a more moist atmosphere. Whatever your environment, be sure the canvas is thoroughly dry before removing the fastenings. I have a gooseneck lamp attached to my desk, which I leave on above my drying needlepoint. This may help speed up the drying time slightly.

Use the palm of your hand to determine if the needlepoint is dry. If the surface feels at all damp or cool, give it more time. If you take up the needlepoint too soon, the dampness will encourage the needlepoint to shift out of shape again.

Removing the Needlepoint from the Blocking Surface

If you have used tacks for blocking, remove these with a screwdriver or blunt kitchen knife. For staples, use the tool at the end of the gun designed expressly for tack removal.

Taking out tacks or staples is more trying than putting them in. I find this job a chore. Once I get into the rhythm of removal it goes quickly, but when I get to a tack or staple that refuses to budge and causes me to break my rhythm, I become annoyed.

Pillow Construction

One of the rewards of needlepoint blocking is that pillow construction for the basic knife-edge pillow is so quick and easy.

Once the needlepoint has been blocked for the final time and you are satisfied that the corners are squared, cut away the masking tape and excess mesh, leaving about 2 rows of canvas on all sides.

Pin the needlepc   face to face with a backing fabric of a similar weight and strength, such as velvet, velveteen or corduroy. Pin as if you were preparing to make any other standard knife-edge pillow. The stitching will be done on the needlepoint side. With your machine, stitch a line of medium-length straight stitches into the needlepoint itself. Place these machine stitches so there is about 1 line of needlepoint stitching on the outside. In other words, you want to construct the pillow so you lose as little of your design as possible but you want to stitch far enough in to give the machine stitching something to grip. As with all other pillows of this type construction, be sure your machine stitching includes all the corners. Leave about 3 inches open in the middle of one side for stuffing. This is larger than is usually necessary, because needlepoint is very bulky.

When the stitching is complete, make the standard diagonal clips in the corners but make sure to cut away only mesh, not stitched canvas! Reverse the pillow and gently free the corners with a crochet hook or blunt end of a pencil. Fill the pillow with Dacron fiberfill and hand stitch closed.

Alternative Backings for Needlepoint

If you find a lightweight fabric in an irresistible color to back your needlepoint, as I did with some beautiful Indian silk, be sure to add a layer of muslin to strengthen the construction. Adding this extra muslin, I have found, will distribute the weight of the needlepoint and enable you to use fabric that might otherwise be too weak. Baste the muslin to the wrong side of the intended fabric with large stitches. Smooth the fabrics flat and then stitch them together diagonally across the center to form an X. Also stitch them together around the edges. Once they are firmly and neatly joined, proceed with the standard construction. When the pillow is constructed, carefully remove any visible basting stitches. Failure to use muslin to strengthen fragile fabrics such as silk or cotton in needle-point pillows will probably result in the ripping of the machine stitching through the weaker fabric.

LIZA NEEDLEPOINT DOLL

The Liza needlepoint doll pillow is a perfect example of needlepoint-on-the-go. I planned the doll on layout paper by drawing and redrawing until I was satisfied with the design. I transferred the design to canvas and bound the raw edges with masking tape. I did not trim the canvas to conform to the doll's shape, however, because I wasn't sure at this early stage whether the finished piece would be a doll-shaped pillow or traditional rectangular-shaped pillow.

I packed a selection of colors from my yarn basket, the canvas with the design, a tapestry needle, and a small pair of scissors into a small bag and tucked the whole "kit" into my handbag. We were on our way to California by plane to visit our newborn niece, Liza. The pillow was to be a gift for her.

I began with the sleeves and bodice of the doll's dress as well as the skirt. I planned to leave the apron until after Liza's name had been stitched. By the time we landed in California, I had made sizable progress. During the 10 days of our visit that followed, I completed the dress, hands, face and feet, leaving the basket, the name, the flowers and the apron.

I put in the name next, adding an extra row of stitching to improve its readability. I felt home free, but I was wrong. There were more problems ahead—but this is all part of the process of designing. Although each design is different, each problem solved is a problem that can be avoided in the future.

Everything was now complete except the flowers, the basket handle and the apron. I experimented with a few approaches to the flowers but, dissatisfied, I removed these attempts. Finally, I decided to treat the canvas as if it were embroidery cloth. Using the basic satin stitch and letting the holes of the needlepoint guide the needle, I put in the flowers and leaves with long and short stitches. I used French knots to fill two of the flower centers. The contrast of the bulky embroidery and the refined needlepoint was very pleasing and gave the doll a slightly three-dimensional quality.

When the flowers were finished, I stitched in the handle of the basket, leaving only the doll's apron to be finished. My supply of white was running low so instead of getting started with what I had and then trying

Circular Needlepoint Sampler, page 95

From left to right: Rainbow Mat and Bolster, page 136

From left to right: Cross-Stitch Pillow for Molly, page 66, Rabbit Ribbon Pillow, page 153, Cross-Stitch Flower Basket, page 63

From left to right: Needlepoint Tree, page 89, Needlepoint Flower Basket, page 105, Liza Needlepoint Doll, page 86, Needlepoint Angel, page 92

From left to right: Patchwork Pie Wedge, page 127, Appliqué Vase of Flowers, page 150

Patchwork Rice-Sack Pillow, page 134

From left to right: Yo-yo Fish Pillow, page 155, Crewel Cat, page 53, Hexagon Pillow, page 130

Camels for Peter, page 200

Ribbon Pillows, page 157

From left to right: Turkish Cushion, page 34,
Turkish Bolster, page 141

Sock Pillows, page 172

Appliqué Family, page 170

From left to right: Purple Pansy, page 102, Polish Flowers, page 107

From left to right: Lace Lady, page 163, Crewel Flower Basket, page 56, Lace Landscape, page 161

Star Pillow page 208

Quilted House, page 184

From left to right: Diagonal Challis Pillow, page 124, Crazy-Quilt Pillow, page 190

From left to right: Crochet Granny Square, page 7, Cross-Stitch Baby Sampler, page 61

From left to right: Fruit Pillows on Velvet, page 202, Needlepoint with Ducks and Rabbits, page 99

to match it, I bought 2 ounces of good quality Persian yarn in off-white.

I put the final stitches into the Liza doll on the return flight to New York. I had decided that the finished pillow would be doll shaped rather than a traditional rectangle so I added extra stitches between the doll's feet and around the outside of the doll. These stitches would be seam allowance when I constructed the pillow.

When I got home, I blocked the doll three times before I was satisfied with the shape.

When the piece was finally in shape, I trimmed off the excess canvas to match the doll's silhouette, leaving a 2-row margin of blank mesh all around.

The final doll pillow was constructed the same as any other knife-edge pillow. I machine stitched around the entire perimeter of the doll into the extra 2 rows I had done beyond the actual doll design. I left about 3 inches open on the doll's skirt for reversing the pillow. When I got to the neck, waist and feet, I clipped away the mesh as close to the stitching as I dared, being extremely careful not to cut into the needlepoint itself or the construction stitching. Because of the bulk of the needlepoint and the velveteen, reversing the doll to expose the right side was slow work. Using a heavy crochet hook as well as my fingers, trying to be as patient as possible (I was anxious to see the finished doll), I finally got the job done. I stuffed her with Dacron fiberfill, using a crochet hook to push it into the head, feet and body. When she was well stuffed but not bulging, I pinned the opening on the side of her skirt and stitched her closed by hand.

Materials Needed:

Finished size: 12½ inches high x 6½ inches wide (at extremes)

Waterproof felt-tipped marker

10-thread-to-the-inch mono needlepoint mesh—14 x 8-inch piece, raw edges bound with masking tape

For continental stitch: 1 ounce of Persian needlepoint yarn for each large area shown, in colors indicated; ½ ounce for all other colors

For basketweave stitch: double yarn amounts

For embroidered flowers: ¼ ounce for each

Tapestry or needlepoint needle for all work

Velveteen or other material of your choice for pillow back—14 x 8 inches (*plus seam allowance*)

Sewing machine (optional—for final construction of pillow)

Pillow stuffing

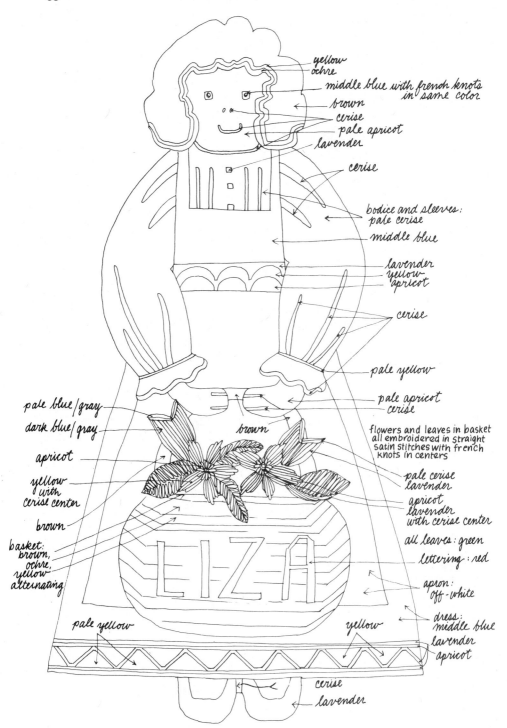

yellow ochre

middle blue with french knots in same color

brown

cerise

pale apricot

lavender

cerise

bodice and sleeves: pale cerise

middle blue

lavender
yellow
apricot

cerise

pale yellow

pale apricot
cerise

pale blue/gray

dark blue/gray

brown

flowers and leaves in basket all embroidered in straight satin stitches with french knots in centers

apricot

yellow with cerise center

pale cerise
lavender

apricot
lavender
with cerise center

brown

all leaves: green

basket:
brown,
ochre,
yellow
alternating

lettering: red

apron:
off-white

pale yellow

yellow

dress:
middle blue
lavender
apricot

cerise

lavender

LIZA

Liza needlepoint doll

To Make This Pillow:

1. Enlarge chart given here to appropriate size according to instructions on page 16.
2. Using marker, trace enlarged drawing onto mesh.
3. Using the colors indicated on the chart, stitch in all areas using continental stitch. Large areas may also be done in basketweave, if preferred.
4. Leave the flowers until last and stitch them with long and short embroidery satin stitches, following the flower outlines as closely as possible.
5. When all stitching is complete, block needlepoint as described on page 81, and finish pillow with knife-edge construction, using velveteen or other material.

NEEDLEPOINT TREE

Once the Liza doll (page 86) was completed, I decided it would be nice to make a needlepoint tree to accompany her. My first impulse was to draw a realistic tree based on one from a natural history book but the more I sketched the more discouraged I became. Finally, I arrived at a drawing that seemed acceptable and I traced it onto canvas. I colored in some of the areas with waterproof markers and began stitching. But the more I stitched, the less enthusiastic I became. Finally the realization hit me. I admire realistic-looking needlepoint done by other people, but for my own work, I prefer more primitive and whimsical motifs. It took me a while to come to this discovery, but in the end I was very relieved. No longer would I try to force myself to do needlework to imitate the work of someone else. You, too, will have to evaluate your own artistic inclinations. If you decide that your heart really is in representational needlepoint, there are ways to achieve these ends using photographs and magazine clippings without being able to draw.

Using graph paper and a dictionary of needlepoint stitches to help plan my pattern, and with my basket of yarn leftovers to supply the colors, I began stitching. I used only simple repeat patterns, although seeing them one next to the other in the finished pillow may make them appear more complicated than they really are.

Because the sides of the tree slope, it will be impossible to end each design exactly in the right place. Besides, you will need extra stitching on the outside of the actual tree for seam allowance. As a result, when making my pillow I stitched right over the borders, and the finished tree (just before pillow construction) looked very misshapen. The base of the tree was stitched with horizontal stripes so there was no problem in keeping the original shape. For your pillow, make sure to stitch several rows beyond the outline to allow for seam allowance in the pillow construction.

When the stitching on the tree is complete, it may be a ragged sight! It's hard to believe that such a helter-skelter looking piece of needlework could ever become a trim, refined tree.

Block the finished needlework twice, using the instructions on page 81. Although one blocking may seem adequate for the top of the tree, the tiny trunk, done in continental stitches, may be so crooked that you will have to block the whole piece a second time.

When the blocking is complete, you are ready to construct the pillow. Pin the tree template to the back of the needlework, centering it carefully so it lines up with the part of the needlework intended for the tree pillow. Then, pin the needlework face to face with velveteen or other backing fabric. Using the template as a guide, machine stitch closely around the edge of the paper shape. Work slowly so as not to sew into the paper or sew too far from its edge. I left the standard 4-inch gap unstitched on the side of the tree for reversing the pillow.

When the stitching is complete, clip away the mesh from the corners of the tree and the trunk and the mesh across the top point of the tree, being careful not to cut into the needlework itself.

This shaped pillow is easier to reverse than the Liza doll because there are no small enclosed areas. The tree is also easy to stuff, once reversed. Pin the remaining opening and hand stitch it closed.

Materials Needed:

Finished size: 10 x 14 inches (at extremes)

10-thread-to-the-inch mono needlepoint mesh—11 x 15-inch piece, raw edges bound with masking tape
Dark waterproof felt-tipped marker
Tapestry needle
1 ounce of Persian needlepoint yarn in each color indicated on chart
Materials listed for blocking needlepoint (see page 81)
Velveteen or fabric of your choice for pillow back—11 x 15-inch (*plus seam allowance*) piece
Sewing machine (optional—for pillow construction)
Pillow stuffing

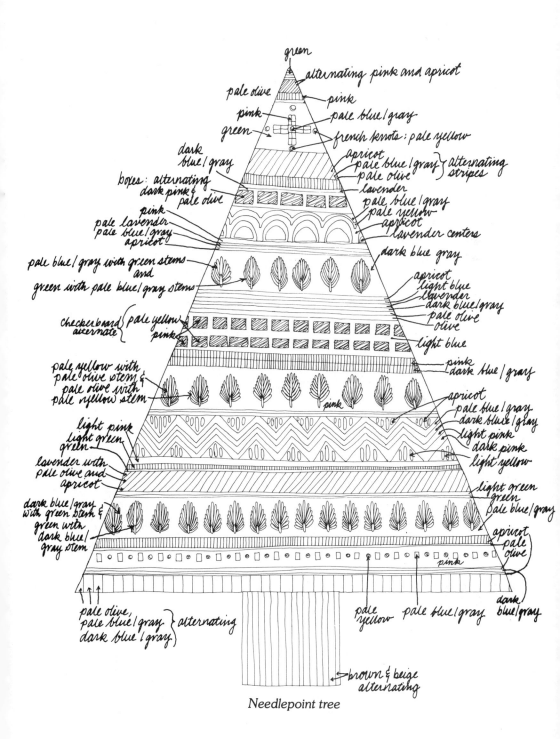

Needlepoint tree

To Make This Pillow:

1. Using one of the methods described on page 16, enlarge outline of tree given here to appropriate size.
2. Using marker, trace the enlarged outline onto mesh.
3. Using colors indicated on chart, stitch in all areas with lines of bargello stitching selected from those pictured on page 91. Use the continental stitch to do all other stitching such as tree trunk, single stitched stripes, diagonals and background for leaf patterns, as shown in color photograph.
4. When all stitching is complete, block needlepoint as described on page 81 and finish pillow in knife-edge construction, using velveteen or other backing fabric.

NEEDLEPOINT ANGEL

I designed and stitched the needlepoint angel for my mother as a Christmas gift several years ago. When Christmas rolled around, the needlepoint was complete but the pillow was not. So, I wrapped the needle-

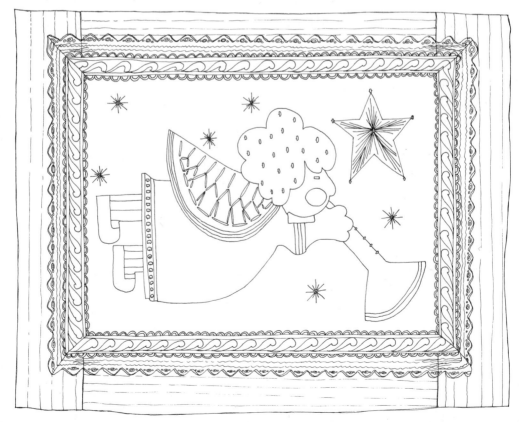

point as it was and presented it to her with the promise of making it into a pillow. The needlepoint was so tiny, however, that for months I resisted completing the pillow for fear it would turn out to be insignificant. Finally, with much trepidation, I decided to add to the needlepoint with ribbon trimming and lace in the hopes of enlarging the surface of the pillow top and improving the stature of the needlework. The process itself was not difficult and the finished pillow has a special new presence. The angel design is 6 x 8 inches, but the finished pillow is 10 x 12 inches. Traditionally formal needlepoint has been joined with the more easy-going patchwork.

I drew the angel design on paper first and then traced it onto 14-thread-to-the-inch mesh, as described on page 78. The original design was made up of simple, flat shapes. But when the needlepoint stitching was complete, I felt the need for more texture. With the same needle and Persian needlepoint yarn, I added embroidery stitches over the angel's wing and the large star. I also added the small embroidered stars and beaded highlights as an afterthought.

Materials Needed:

Finished size: 10 x 12 inches
Needlepoint panel: 6 x 8 inches plus 2-inch patchwork borders

Waterproof felt-tipped marker
14-thread-to-the-inch mono needlepoint canvas—8 x 10-inch piece, raw
    edges bound with masking tape
For continental stitch, the following amounts of Persian needlepoint yarn
    for each color shown in drawing: ½ ounce for angel's body, ¼ ounce
    for all smaller areas, 2 ounces for background
For basketweave stitch: double yarn amounts
For embroidery stitching: approximately 1 yard of Persian needlepoint
    yarn (available by the strand at needlepoint shops)
Tapestry needle
Two small packages of pastel glass beads (available in hobby shops)
Sewing needle and thread
45 inches of 2-inch-wide gingham satin acetate ribbon (*plus seam allow-
    ance*) or material of your choice for patchwork borders, plus 45 inches
    of 2-inch-wide lace
Materials listed on page 81 for blocking needlepoint
10 x 12-inch (*plus seam allowance*) piece of velveteen or fabric of your
    choice for pillow back
Sewing machine (optional)
Pillow stuffing

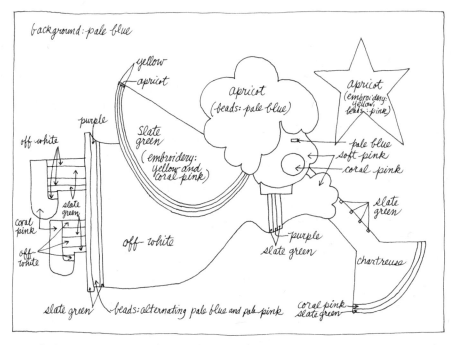

background: pale blue

yellow
apricot
purple
off white
slate green
(embroidery: yellow and coral pink)
apricot
(beads: pale blue)
apricot
(embroidery: yellow; beads: pink)
pale blue
soft pink
coral pink
coral pink
slate green
off white
off white
slate green
purple
slate green
chartreuse
off white
slate green
beads: alternating pale blue and pale pink
coral pink
slate green

Embroidery stitch and bead placement indicated above, shown in previous drawing.
Embroidered stars shown there are done in yellow with pink beads.

To Make This Pillow:

1. Using one of the methods described on pages 16–18, enlarge drawing given here to appropriate size.
2. Using marker, trace enlarged outline onto mesh (*plus seam allowance*).
3. Using colors indicated on chart, stitch in areas using the continental stitch. Use the basketweave for background, if preferred. Use 2 strands of needlepoint yarn by removing 1 strand from the standard 3-strand yarn.
4. When needlepoint is complete, block according to instructions on page 81.
5. When blocking is complete, add embroidery satin stitches inside of large star and angel wings with 2 strands of needlepoint yarn. Add small stars with satin stitching according to color and placement indicated on drawing.

6. Add beads using standard sewing needle and thread. Knot thread on back after each bead is added.
7. Add patchwork border of ribbon or fabric of choice, as described on page 119.
8. Pin and appliqué old lace in place over completed patchwork border, using small hand stitching.
9. Complete pillow in knife-edge construction (page 25), using velveteen or other backing fabric.

CIRCULAR NEEDLEPOINT SAMPLER

Dorothy Globus's circular needlepoint sampler (shown in the color section), filled with color and pattern, looks different every time I see it. I was so excited by the images the first time I saw it that it became the inspiration for my own patchwork needlepoint on page 99. My one patchwork pillow hasn't been enough. I feel inspired to do another whenever I see Dorothy's pillow. I hope seeing it here will have the same effect on you.

When I asked Dorothy about the development of the pillow, she told me it was her first experience with needlepoint! I was amazed, yet the more we talked about the pillow, the more I began to see that it had evolved slowly and naturally through Dorothy's desire to experiment and create a pillow that was completely personal.

Dorothy began by stitching random patterns in the mesh, but she quickly realized that she needed a unifying element to hold all of the designs together. By this time she had discovered that geometric shapes were perfectly suited to the evenly spaced mesh. This led her to the idea of stitching an overall grid of boxes in the mesh and putting a different stitch design in each box.

Experimenting and finally discovering the usefulness of the grid was the hardest part of the design process. Once Dorothy had set up her system, the stitchery was a pleasure.

Since this was her first time with needlepoint, Dorothy learned more and more about the stitches and materials as she worked. She began with a few bargello or thread-count designs in which she developed a repeating pattern by drawing straight stitches over several threads of the mesh at one time. This stitch may look complicated but it is so similar to the satin stitch done in embroidery that one does it almost instinctively. She placed these designs in random boxes within the grid, feeling her way carefully as she stitched.

By the time she had completed a few boxes with geometric patterns, she was ready to experiment with pictorial images. Using a basic continental stitch (although she didn't know it was called that at the time) she developed many engaging motifs. Among my favorites are: a house, an owl, a clock, a sailboat, a duck, a tree, a carrot and a whale. She also included portraits of herself and her husband Stephen.

Dorothy worked on her pillow over summer weekends at the beach. She loved doing this project so much that she made herself a needlepoint belt, similar to the gusset. She has charted many of the motifs for you to use, but try to include some personal variations in your own sampler. To copy the pictorial designs, use the continental stitch described on page 73. To do the bargello patterns, do straight stitches, working as if you were doing the embroidered satin stitches described on page 50. Dorothy used 2 strands of 3-strand Persian needlepoint yarn, and the pillow is backed with dark green velvet.

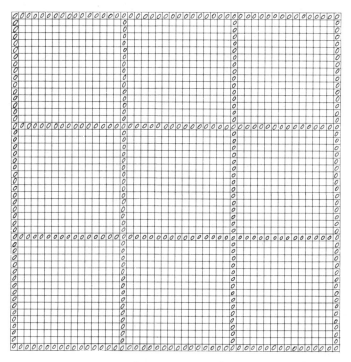

Setting up a grid

Materials Needed:

Finished size: 13½ inches across

Persian needlepoint yarn—½ ounce in each of at least twelve colors. Use photograph in color section as a guide in your color choice. Be sure to use a dark color such as olive green or brown for the lines of the grid and clear, bright colors for all other stitching.

14-thread-to-the-inch mono needlepoint canvas—15 x 15-inch piece, and 15 x 14-inch strip for gusset, raw edges bound with masking tape

Dark waterproof felt-tipped marker

Circular template with 13½-inch diameter. Use dinner plate or other ready-made circle, or draft your own with a compass on cardboard.

Tapestry needle

Materials for blocking needlepoint (see page 81)

Flannel, corduroy or other fabric for pillow back—one piece 15 x 15 inches (*plus seam allowance*)

Sewing machine (optional)

Pillow stuffing

To Make This Pillow:

1. Using marker, center and trace a circle onto mesh.
2. Use the continental stitch to stitch straight lines from right to left and then top to bottom to set up a grid of boxes over the entire surface of circle. (See page 80 for instructions on reading stitch charts.) Each box should measure 18 stitches by 18 stitches. Do not stop stitching at edge of circular outline. Instead, extend over the outlines by a few stitches to act as seam allowance. Work until entire surface is covered with grid.
3. Stitch geometric bargello patterns and representational pictures into each box of the grid. Use designs shown on pages 99 as a guide. Placement of designs and pictures should be random but pleasing to your eye.
4. Stitch until all boxes are filled with pattern and entire circle (*plus seam allowance*) is covered with stitching.
5. To make needlepoint gusset, use strip of needlepoint mesh. Set up grid of approximately 40 boxes of 18 x 18 stitches plus extra stitches as seam allowance as directed for face of pillow. (Or, you can use a strip of plain, heavy fabric of your choice.)
6. Fill these boxes with bargello patterns and pictures in same style as pillow face. Repeat favorite patterns, if desired.

7. Block finished needlepoint pillow top and gusset according to instructions on page 81.
8. With dressmaker's chalk, trace circular template used for original circle over needlepoint on *wrong* side of stitching to indicate stitch line for pillow construction.
9. Construct pillow as box pillow according to description on page 30.

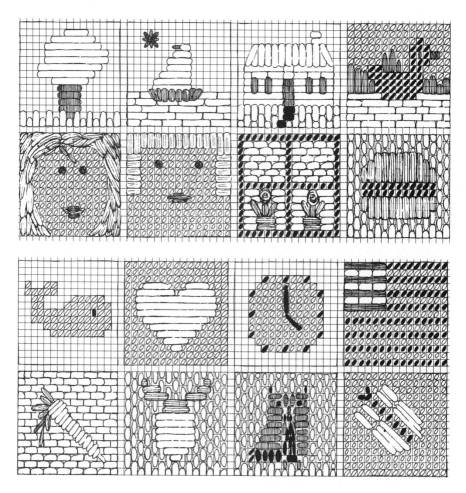

Pictorial improvisations from the circular needlepoint sampler

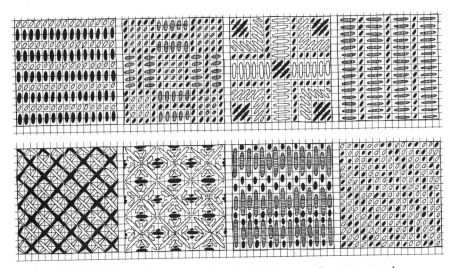

Geometric improvisations from the circular needlepoint sampler

Bargello setups to use as an aid when improvising

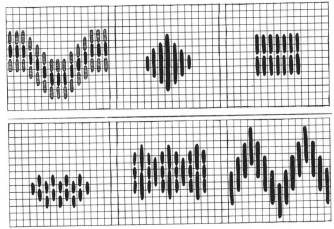

PATCHWORK NEEDLEPOINT WITH DUCKS
AND RABBITS

This pillow (shown in color section) was inspired by Dorothy Globus's circular needlepoint sampler on page 95. I became so excited looking at all the inventive patterns and pictures that I decided to try the improvisational method myself. Armed with a swatch from my recently upholstered couch, I went to my favorite needlepoint store and chose several ounces of wool to match the colors in the fabric. The rest of the Persian yarn would come from leftovers from previous projects. I could have made the pillow entirely from these scraps without any additional purchases but I bought the new yarn in the same colors as the couch so I would be sure that the finished design would coordinate.

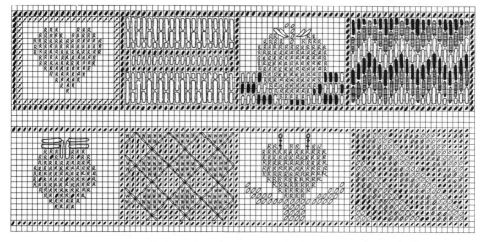

Bargello and pictorial boxes from patchwork needlepoint with ducks and rabbits

Materials Needed:

Finished size: 13 x 16½ inches

Dark waterproof felt-tipped marker
10-thread-to-the-inch mono needlepoint canvas—one 15 x 18-inch piece, raw edges bound with masking tape
For continental stitch: ½ ounce Persian needlepoint wool for each color listed on chart, plus 1 ounce for each color used in duck and rabbit backgrounds and areas inside triangles
Tapestry needle
Materials for blocking needlepoint (see page 81)
Velveteen or other fabric for pillow back—one piece 13 x 16½ inches (*plus seam allowance*)
Sewing machine (optional)
Pillow stuffing

Half the chart for the patchwork needlepoint with ducks and rabbits

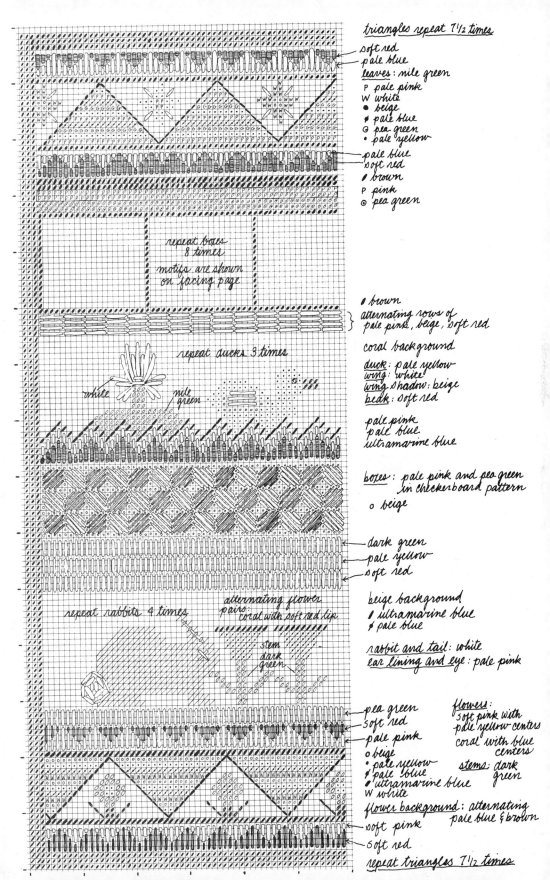

triangles repeat 7½ times

soft red
pale blue
leaves: nile green
P pale pink
W white
• beige
✚ pale blue
G pea green
• pale yellow

pale blue
soft red
ı brown
P pink
◎ pea green

repeat boxes
8 times

motifs are shown
on facing page

ı brown
alternating rows of
pale pink, beige, soft red

coral background

duck: pale yellow
wing: white
wing shadow: beige
beak: soft red

pale pink
pale blue
ultramarine blue

repeat ducks 3 times

white

nile
green

boxes: pale pink and pea green
in checkerboard pattern

o beige

dark green
pale yellow
soft red

beige background
ı ultramarine blue
✚ pale blue

rabbit and tail: white
ear lining and eye: pale pink

repeat rabbits 4 times

alternating flower
pairs: coral with soft red lip

stem
dark
green

pea green
soft red
pale pink
o beige
• pale yellow
✚ pale blue
• ultramarine blue
W white

flowers:
soft pink with
pale yellow centers
coral with blue
centers
stems: dark
green

flower background: alternating
pale blue & brown
soft pink
soft red

repeat triangles 7½ times

To Make This Pillow:

1. Using marker, line off a 13 x 16½ inch rectangle on needlepoint mesh.
2. Using charts as well as color photograph, count and copy stitches shown. All single stitching is continental, but for background areas, basketweave may also be used. To do bargello, carry your yarn over several lines of mesh at a time, as shown on charts. (See page 80 for instructions on reading stitch charts.)
3. To simplify work, choose one horizontal motif such as ducks or checkerboard pattern and complete the entire stripe containing this design before going on to another.
4. Complete stitching in sequence described in step 3 or in any sequence that is satisfying.
5. When stitching is complete, block needlepoint according to instructions on page 81 and construct as knife-edge pillow, using 13 x 16½ inch velvet *plus seam allowance* as pillow back.

PURPLE PANSY

The purple pansy was one of Miriam Ress's earliest creations, done many years ago before needlepoint became as popular as it is today. The fact that it looks so freshly designed and inventively stitched is a credit to Miriam's strong design sense and painterly instinct with needle and yarn. When I asked her about this pillow, Miriam told me that she knew what she wanted her flower to look like but she had someone else draw the basic flower shape on the 14-lines-to-the-inch canvas. She could have easily traced it herself from a picture book of flowers but, like many good needleworkers who have specific design ideas, she felt timid about working out the actual details. A few people like Miriam are lucky enough to have someone nearby who is available to help; others are not so fortunate. Yet, people who have strong design ideas are more than capable of preparing their own needlework. The missing ingredient here is confidence, an intangible and often elusive quality.

It is hard to believe that the purple pansy was stitched by a person with little needlepoint experience, but even as a beginner Miriam allowed herself the freedom to improvise. She decided on her large color areas, which were outlined on the canvas, but she wanted her flower to be soft edged in the way of a real flower, so instead of making each petal a solid color, hard edged shape, she used thread blends in her needle to stitch in primitive but effective shading. The areas of color appear almost ran-

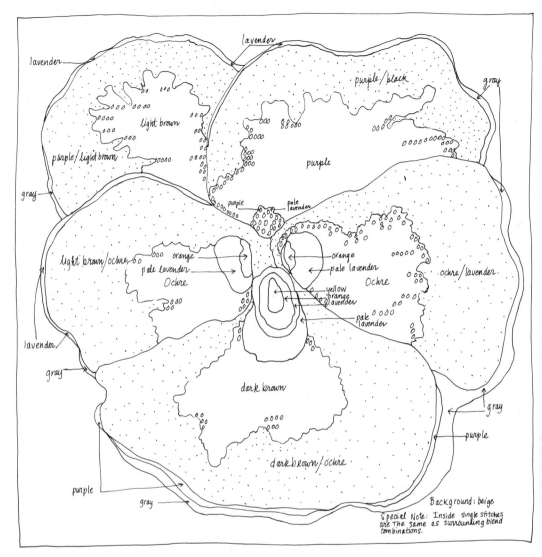

Outline and color placement for purple pansy pillow

dom, but you can create the same effect by studying the photograph in the color section and placing your stitches within the shapes defined in the drawing included here.

To make your own pansy, use Miriam's color combinations or create your own with what you have in your scrap basket. The soft white background Miriam used for her pillow is in sharp contrast to the strong, dark flower shape, making the flower image even more powerful seen from a distance.

The finished pillow has a beige silk backing and is a simple knife-edge shape.

Materials Needed:

Finished size: 11 x 11 inches

Dark waterproof felt-tipped marker

14-thread-to-the-inch mono needlepoint canvas—one piece 13 x 13 inches, raw edges bound with masking tape

For continental stitch: 2-ounce skeins of Persian yarn in colors shown in drawing; 2 ounces of eggshell white. For red and yellow pansy center you will need ½ ounce of each color.

For basketweave stitch: double yarn amounts

Tapestry needle

Materials for blocking needlepoint (see page 81)

Silk, or fabric of your choice, for pillow back—one piece 11 x 11 inches (*plus seam allowance*)

Sewing machine (optional)

Pillow stuffing

To Make This Pillow:

1. Using marker, line off 11 x 11-inch rectangle on 14-lines-to-the-inch mono canvas. Bind off raw edges with masking tape to prevent raveling.
2. Enlarge drawing on page 103 to appropriate size according to instructions on page 16.
3. Darken lines of enlarged drawing with heavy line. Place face up on table. Tape mesh over drawing and trace outline through onto mesh within the marked boundaries, using waterproof marker.
4. Use only 2 strands of Persian yarn paired in color combinations shown in chart. Fill in each area of pansy with the continental stitch. Do not be afraid to allow each area to take on a softened random edge, as this will contribute to the effectiveness of the flowers.
5. Use 2 ounces of eggshell white to complete pansy background. Basketweave stitching may be used here but this will double the amount of wool needed.
6. Block completed needlepoint according to instructions on page 81.
7. Complete in knife-edge construction as described on page 25, using silk with muslin or whatever your fabric choice as a reinforcing second layer, cut to 11 x 11 inches (*plus seam allowance*) for pillow backing.

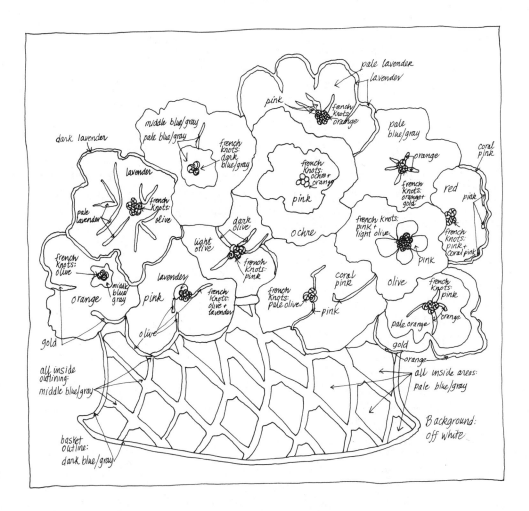

NEEDLEPOINT FLOWER BASKET

The needlepoint flower basket was designed and stitched by Miriam Ress in 1964, well before needlepoint became popular. Although the flower-basket motif has since become a favorite of needlepointers, Miriam's simple, whimsical shapes and soft, sophisticated colors have kept her design looking fresh and original.

I have included here an outline drawing of Miriam's pillow as well as color notations. At first glance, this pillow seems to be stitched with only a few simple candy colors but when I began to count them, comparing shades from flower to flower, I realized that this pillow (as the others presented here by Miriam Ress) was done in the best tradition of improvisation. Miriam used what she had in her yarn basket and in using so many slightly different shades of yarn has created a subtle glow over the whole surface. The mesh she used is 14-lines-to-the-inch and the small stitching required to cover this size canvas has also allowed her to add delicate highlights and details to her flowers, which would not have been possible with a coarser canvas. The flower centers are filled with tiny French knots. Use Miriam's colors or draw your own combinations from your yarn basket. As with the purple pansy on page 103, Miriam used a soft white background to set off the strong solid shape of the flower basket.

This is a knife-edge pillow backed with soft green velvet.

Materials Needed:

Finished size: 10 x 10 inches

Waterproof felt-tipped marker
12 x 12-inch 14-lines-to-the-inch mono needlepoint canvas, raw edges bound with masking tape
For continental stitch: Persian yarn for needlepoint in the following amounts: 1 ounce in each color shown plus 2 ounces of main color and 2½ ounces for background, and 5 or 6 strands in colors shown for French knots
For basketweave: double all amounts
Tapestry needle
Materials listed on page 81 for blocking needlepoint
10 x 10-inch velvet *plus seam allowance,* or other fabric for pillow back
Sewing machine (optional)
Pillow stuffing

To Make This Pillow:

1. Using marker, line off 10 x 10 inches on canvas.
2. Enlarge drawing on page 105 to appropriate size according to instructions on page 16.
3. Darken outline of enlarged drawing with heavy line. Place face up on table. Tape needlepoint mesh over drawing and trace outline onto mesh within the marked boundaries, using waterproof marker.

4. Use Persian yarn and choose an assortment of pastel colors in 1-ounce amounts according to those shown on page 105. For flower basket, you will need 2 ounces of wool in the color you choose to predominate (pale gray-blue, as shown here) and 2½ ounces for the background (off-white).
5. With 2 strands of the normally 3-strand yarn in your tapestry needle, use the continental stitch to fill in each area, as shown on page 73. If you use the basketweave stitch, be sure to double the amount of wool needed.
6. When needlepoint is completed, add French knots to the center of each flower in colors indicated.
7. Block completed needlepoint according to instructions on page 81.
8. Complete in knife-edge construction as described on page 25, using velvet measuring 10 x 10 inches *plus seam allowance* for pillow backing.

POLISH FLOWERS

This pillow by Miriam Ress was inspired by a warm, rich Polish rug in her foyer. Although the rug was woven on a tapestry loom, and the pillow stitched on needlepoint mesh, Miriam was able to capture the softness prevalent in Polish weaves by threading two colors of yarn into her needle. The result is a surprising tweed effect that is rarely seen in needlepoint.

This project is a perfect example of needlepoint-on-the-go. Miriam assembled her materials into a small bag for a vacation in Mexico. The canvas is very small, so much of the stitching was done on the plane.

She stitched the flowers and stems first, using a mixture of continental and basketweave. The beauty of this pillow is its spontaneity.

Assemble an assortment of Persian yarn, and twist pairs of colors together in your needle. Keep your foreground shapes light and bright and your background colors dark. To blend colors successfully, choose two colors that are similar in value. Colors that appear almost indistinguishable in your hand produce a delicate texture when stitched together.

Although Miriam's pillow is finished with a standard knife edge, the backing material is very special. Miriam chose a butter-soft dark brown suede. A surprising choice and it works beautifully. You, too, can back your pillows with soft, thin suede or leather. All you need is a heavy-duty needle in your machine, available in sewing supply stores. Find suede in hobby shops or look in the phone book under ''suede'' and ''leather.'' A local clothing manufacturer may give or sell you scraps.

Polish flowers

Materials Needed:

Finished size: 9½ x 9½ inches

Waterproof felt-tipped marker
12 x 12-inch 14-thread-to-the-inch mono needlepoint canvas, raw edges
bound with masking tape
For continental stitch: Persian yarn—about ½ ounce of each color
shown on chart
For basketweave stitch: double yarn amounts
Tapestry needle
Materials listed on page 81 for blocking needlepoint
9½ x 9½-inch (*plus seam allowance*) soft brown suede or velvet or other
fabric for pillow back
Sewing machine (optional)
Pillow stuffing

To Make This Pillow:

1. Using marker, line off 9½ x 9½ inches on canvas.
2. Enlarge drawing to appropriate size according to instructions on page
   16.
3. Darken outline of enlarged drawing with heavy line. Place face up on
   table. Tape needlepoint mesh over drawing and trace outline onto
   mesh within the marked boundaries, using marker.
4. With 2 strands of yarn paired in color combinations listed, fill in each
   flower and stem, using the continental stitch. Do not be afraid to allow
   each area to vary slightly from the outline given, as softened edges
   will contribute to the effectiveness of the shapes.
5. When the flower shapes are completed, add the background stitching
   also by pairing together 2 colors of wool. Use the drawn boundaries
   as a basic guide but, again, do not be afraid to deviate. Refer to the
   photo in the color section.
6. When needlepoint is completed, block according to instructions on
   page 81.
7. Complete in knife-edge construction as described on page 25, using
   very soft suede (with heavy-duty needle in your sewing machine) or
   velvet measuring 9½ x 9½ inches (*plus seam allowance*) for pillow
   backing.

Polish flowers   *Flowers with random thread-blend background*

 **SEVEN**

Patchwork

PATCHWORK TECHNIQUES

Patchwork is the technique of joining small pieces of fabric together with seams to make a larger unit. Although the simplest units are the square, the rectangle and the hexagon, many patchwork patterns are a sophisticated arrangement of these elements, which are then sewn together to form a square. Repeating squares are then sewn together to form a larger geometric surface. These large pieces are generally used to make a quilt or comforter, but smaller units are great for pillow making.

Patchwork and pillows work well together, especially for beginners. The construction of the patchwork pillow top is almost identical to the construction of a patchwork quilt top. The patchwork quilt top can become unwieldy and hard to maneuver but a patchwork pillow, usually lap sized, is easy to handle.

Patchwork pillows have a special decorative quality and are surprisingly quick and inexpensive to make. The novice who has successfully completed a patchwork pillow will have a delightful decorating accessory and will be better prepared to undertake a more challenging quilt. (For details on how to make patchwork items, please see my book *The Patchwork Point of View,* Simon and Schuster, New York, New York, 1975).

Although patchwork can involve an intricate arrangement of shapes, the shapes used to create the patchwork pillows in the following section are so simple that they are appropriate to the most inexperienced newcomer. The construction and sewing are so straightforward that most of the pillows can be put together in an evening.

If this is your first sewing experience, consider completing a small patchwork pillow top by hand. Although a sewing machine is faster, you will have more control if you use hand stitches. This will be especially important if you make the hexagon pillow on page 133. The larger projects such as the rainbow pillow and bolster beginning on page 137 should be done by machine because they are meant for heavy-duty use. Pillow constructions, where possible, should be done by machine.

Special note: One would assume, since I recommend that beginners work by hand, that this stitching is not as desirable as machine stitching. The truth is that hand stitching, while not as fast or sturdy, is infinitely more beautiful and delicate.

Aside from the patchwork pillows that follow, many pillows in this collection have been made larger by the addition of patchwork borders. Any piece of fabric or needlework can be extended this way, but choose your patchwork borders with care. Thoughtfully combined prints, textures and stitchery enhance each other while ill-chosen combinations can cancel each other out. When adding patchwork borders to a pillow, follow the same principles that you would for any patchwork project according to the information that follows.

*Materials for patchwork,
appliqué and quilting*

BASIC SUPPLIES FOR PATCHWORK, APPLIQUÉ AND QUILTING

Thread

For all-purpose machine and hand sewing, use mercerized, bel-waxed cotton thread. This is not so easy to find since most notion counters are loaded with polyester thread. I find polyester to be hard on my hands as well as difficult to regulate in my sewing machine. Admittedly, I can't always find cotton thread in the colors I need, so I do sometimes use synthetic. Occasionally I find a sewing shop or five-and-ten that is clearing out its supply of old cotton thread. On these occasions I have bought as much as I could afford, no matter how unusual the color. Usually these discontinued spools also have discontinued prices (those made just three or four years ago were priced originally at a much lower rate than those available today) so I feel that I'm getting a bargain all around.

For quilting, use special quilting thread, which is heavy-duty waxed cotton. Most often available in white, some stores carry it in a variety of colors. Today, it's easier to find in local shops than it was several years ago, but if you can't find it near you, order it through the mail. See page 212.

Scissors

Good sharp scissors are your best friend when working with patchwork and appliqué. Clean edges and accurate corners are important to successful assembly of materials. You will be frustrated and misled into thinking patchwork is difficult if you use poor shears. Invest in a good pair with nine-inch blades and save them for cutting fabrics only. Hide them from your roommate, children or spouse, if necessary!

Small embroidery scissors are handy to have for trimming threads and other small cuts.

You will also need a pair of all-purpose scissors for cutting templates, paper patterns and anything else. This is the pair to lend when scissors are requested.

Pins

Use medium-weight straight pins with small glass heads because they are easy to handle and do not leave huge gouges in fabric. Periodically discard any bent pins. They are only a nuisance.

Pincushion

A pincushion will make your pins more manageable, although glass-headed pins usually come in a small plastic box, which is fine.

Thimble

A thimble can feel like an extra finger but there will be times when you'll be glad to have one on. Use a thimble to protect your fingers when you are stitching through several layers of fabric. Thimbles come in a variety of sizes, so when buying one, try on a few until you find one that fits snugly without pinching.

Needles

Needles come in such a range of sizes and shapes it can be hard to choose the right one for each job. For patchwork, appliqué and quilting, use a "between"-size needle (usually numbered from 7 to 10). These betweens are tiny and they may feel awkward at first, especially if you are used to doing needlepoint or crewel, but the delicate point will glide easily through layers of cotton fabric.

Marking Tools

A medium lead pencil is good for all marking on fabric as well as on paper.

Tailor's chalk is also good. It comes in a variety of shades so you may use it on a fabric too dark for pencil.

Dressmaker's carbon can also be useful for appliqué. If you plan to make pillows from commercial patterns (such as the pie wedge on page 127), you will need a package of dressmaker's carbon as well as a tracing wheel.

Templates

A template is the cardboard pattern used in patchwork and appliqué. If you are going to trace your template only a few times, lightweight board such as blotter paper, index card, stock or shirt cardboard is excellent. Whatever paper you use, it should be able to maintain sharp corners and edges long enough for you to trace around it accurately. For bigger projects it is sometimes necessary to make replacement templates. Some people prefer to use sandpaper, rough side down, because it grips fabric firmly.

Draw your template directly on any of these materials and cut out the drafted shape using a utility knife, single edge razor blade and metal ruler.

Or, if you prefer, draft your shape first on graph paper and transfer it to a stiffer surface with carbon between the original and the board. Again, use a metal ruler, pencil and straight blade for accuracy.

An accurate template is very important to the success of your patchwork. A well executed template will produce even patchwork elements. Uneven patchwork elements produce lopsided patchwork pillows.

You will need a ruler to make an accurate square or rectangular template. You may also need an inexpensive compass for hexagons.

Iron

Keep an iron handy so you can press all fabrics for patchwork, appliqué and quilting before you begin work. In most instances, you will have to use your iron several times during the sewing process also, but if your fabric isn't smooth when you begin work, you will have trouble making accurate tracings, cuts and hems.

Always use a press cloth between your fabric and your iron to prevent scorching, especially if your iron isn't Teflon coated.

When working with patchwork and appliqué, use steam to remove old creases and put in new hems. For best results, keep a spray can of water nearby.

Fabrics

Most of the patchwork, appliqué and quilting projects in this book are made from medium-weave prints, plaids, checks and solid color cotton fabric. Cotton is a beautiful, durable, easy-to-handle natural fiber. Unfortunately it is also hard to find and is usually expensive. Wherever possible I go out of my way to use 100 percent cotton for my patchwork and appliqué projects.

Polyester, the most common fabric, is now available in prints, ginghams and plaids that look very much like cotton, but this is where the similarity ends. Polyester doesn't handle or wear like cotton. It won't hold a sharp crease, which is so important in patchwork and appliqué, and it pills and shreds soon after a project is finished. There are many fabrics that are a combination of cotton and synthetic fiber and while these aren't ideal, they are often adequate provided there is mostly cotton in the blend.

How to Recognize Cotton

The most obvious way to recognize cotton is to look for a marking along the selvage edge of the fabric. If no mark is visible (or if, for instance, you are using a scrap with no selvage) look at a cut edge of the fabric to determine the fiber. Pure cotton will have a fuzzy, frayed edge; pure polyester will have a sharp edge from which the fibers fall off in single strands. Blended fabrics will have edges that look like a combination of these, depending on the proportions. A hot iron will stick to the surface of polyester fabric. The idea to keep in mind is that plastic materials will work up into plastic-looking pillows. Personal, creative needlework deserves more respect than this.

Collecting and Using Scrap Fabric

I have been able to make most of my pillows from scrap fabrics left over from sewing projects; you may be able to do this too. If you have no sewing leftovers, there are other places you might look for material. Old clothes, such as lightweight blouses, pajamas and dresses, are often ideal. Old curtains, bedspreads or slipcovers are other possibilities. Choices are endless, provided you follow a few basic principles:

1. Use only fabric that is in good condition. Rotted, old material will not last long enough to justify your time.
2. In patchwork, combine fabrics that are approximately the same weight. Badly balanced patchwork elements will not wear well.
3. Whenever possible, cut patchwork pieces in line with the grain of the fabric.

Buying Fabric

There have been times when I couldn't find materials among my scraps that were just right for a project I was planning. Other times I had one length of fabric in my collection that I wanted to use but I needed companion patterns to round out a project. This is when I have bought fabric. But, in addition to this, I am an incurable browser, and fabric stores are among my favorite haunts. Fortunately, a small amount of fabric can go far in the world of pillow stitchery.

If you are planning a pillow project and decide to buy fabric, there are many places to look. For bargains, consider the small, out-of-the-way yard goods shops. Many of these stores have a comprehensive selection of printed cotton, excellent for patchwork and appliqué. For more sophisticated looking pillows (such as the diagonal patchwork on page 124 and the crazy-quilt pillow on page 191) look for printed wool challis. Also check out the available corduroy, velvet and velveteens for pillow backs. These stores generally carry pillow stuffing (see page 20) and other sewing supplies.

Special note: Don't automatically assume that these places undersell. Comparison shop for price and selection before making any major purchases.

The five-and-ten is also a good place to shop for cotton fabric, although this can be seasonal. Local variety stores usually build up their stock of lightweight fabric in the spring and summer months, but be patient when shopping in these places. Most five-and-tens pile stacks of assorted remnants on a counter and, before long, customers have transformed these piles into a confused mass. I have found some of my favorite fabrics amidst this kind of chaos and so, for me, the patience has paid off. These remnants are often slightly damaged, so check each piece before you buy it to find the imperfection. It may be in an inconspicuous spot near an edge, which is fine, but if the fabric is badly disfigured, reject it.

Department stores often have good fabric departments. Patchwork and appliqué have become so popular that these stores are beginning to carry a large selection of printed cotton as well as other interesting fabrics.

For help in choosing colors, see page 13.

New Pillows from Old Patches

Many a patchwork quilt has been started but never completed. The individual squares for these projects, often stitched in intricate arrangements with beautiful fabrics, are sometimes available in antique shops or at yard sales. This old needlework may be musty with age but most can be revitalized in a gentle bath of soap and water. These squares can be real treasures if you stitch them into simple knife-edged pillows.

DESIGNING SIMPLE PATCHWORK

Designing a patchwork pillow top can be as basic as choosing fabrics and arranging them harmoniously within a grid. All the patchwork pillows presented here were done this way.

To experiment with basic patchwork arrangements, draw a large square over graph paper and divide the square into equal-size smaller squares. Or, fold a square piece of paper into equal square sections. Even in doing this you will have to make choices that will influence the look of the finished pillow. Use colored pencils, pens or crayons to mark off different arrangements of squares. If you prefer, use a pencil and indicate the placement of different printed fabrics with dots, triangles, flowers or any other notations. Try several arrangements. When you have a sketch that you like, decide on the size for your increment (you may be working with paper the actual size of your finished pillow or you may be working just for arrangement with small paper). A pillow of 3 x 3-inch squares placed four across and four down will measure 12 x 12 inches when finished.

To add interest to the design, consider adding strips of patchwork borders in coordinating colors or patterns around the outside edge of a patchwork center.

Using a pencil, ruler and stiff board, draft the template (or templates) for your square module as well as for the border strip. Complete the pillow according to the procedure that follows.

For more difficult patchwork patterns, look through some of the books listed on page 214.

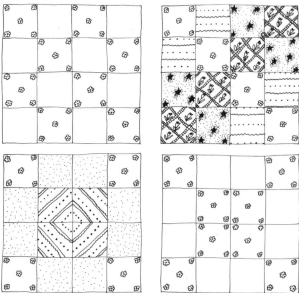

Simple patchwork variations on a grid of 16 squares through placement of printed fabrics

1

2

Adding patchwork borders

1. *Patchwork strips on top and bottom (Be sure to add seam allowances on all sides.)*

2. *Patchwork strip added on each side*

3. *Patchwork strips on top and bottom*

4. *Patchwork strip added on each side*

3

4

PATCHWORK PROCEDURE

Whether you are making a pillow top or a quilt, the steps for basic patchwork are the same. Use the following outline to create your own patchwork, and for variations read through the pillow projects that follow.

1. Chart out your complete patchwork design on paper as described on page 18. Make color and fabric notations on this plan and gather the appropriate fabrics.
2. Cut a separate template for each basic module within your patchwork plan. If your plan contains nine 2-inch squares, you will need to cut only one 2-inch square template, which you will trace 9 times.
3. Press all of the materials that you intend to use in your pillow on the wrong side *before* you begin to work, and continue to press your fabric as needed to keep your project under control.
4. Place your pressed fabric on a hard surface with the wrong side up. Hold the template firmly in place on the fabric with one hand and trace around it with a soft pencil or chalk. Position the template so it is in line with the grain of the fabric. This will prevent the fabric from pulling out of shape later when all of the increments are joined. Trace the template as many times as necessary to fulfill your plan.
5. Trace and cut the fabric economically so a minimum of fabric will be wasted. Cut out the patchwork pieces ¼ inch from the template outline. This extra fabric will be the seam allowance.

    Use the charted plan to make sure you have cut the right number of pieces in the right colors. Refer to this chart often as you work to make sure you are joining the right fabrics in the right positions.
6. Lay out all of your patchwork elements in exact position, right side up. Don't be alarmed at how large an area they cover. The finished pillow will be much smaller once the seam allowances have been used.
7. Sew the pieces together two at a time, using a tiny hand running stitch or a medium machine stitch. To do this, remove two adjoining shapes from your layout, register them carefully face to face with straight pins and sew along one seam. (See next section for details on pinning and sewing.) Take a backstitch at the beginning and end of each sewing line for strength. Press the sewn pair open on the wrong side with both seam allowances lying to one side. Place this pair back in your layout and remove two more.
8. Join all possible pairs together and then sew these pairs to each other to form strips. If you are working with an odd number of increments you may not always be able to work with pairs, but

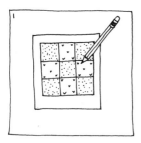

Chart the plan

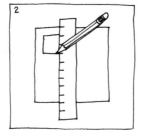

Draw a template on lightweight cardboard

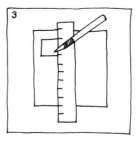

Cut the template using a utility knife and ruler

Press all fabric

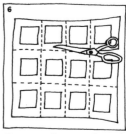

Trace the template onto the wrong side of fabric

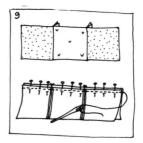

Cut out the patchwork pieces

Place the patchwork pieces in their layout, face up

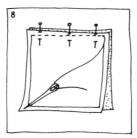

Align and sew pieces together 2 at a time

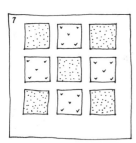

Sew together strips of patchwork to form blocks

choose pairs as long as possible and then add the extra single units.

9. Continue to press after each new addition. Apply a steam iron to the wrong side and push both seam allowances to one side. There are different theories about the correct position of the seam allowance. Some patchworkers feel that the seams should be pressed open. Whichever feels more comfortable to you, the important aspect is that this pressing be gentle. Do not pull your patchwork pieces so firmly that you reveal the stitches. Especially with hand sewing, if the stitches are visible, they are being strained.

10. Finally, join the strips together in the same way, two at a time, to form a larger unit. Carefully align all of these strips with pins before doing final sewing.

11. If you have included any patchwork borders in your design, add these next, using the same method to align them to the patchwork center. Pin them carefully as you would any other patchwork increment and sew them in position. (Note: If these borders are being added to an existing piece of needlepoint, use a sewing machine for a strong seam. Patchwork borders for embroidery such as the crewel cat or crewel flower basket (pages 53 and 56) or cross-stitched flower basket or sampler (pages 63 and 61) may be done by hand, although the machine is faster.)

Add as many patchwork borders as you feel necessary to enhance your design in whatever width of fabrics look best to you.

12. When your design is complete, press again on the wrong side and proceed with the final pillow construction.

REGISTERING PATCHWORK INCREMENTS WITH PINS

It is imperative that you register your patchwork elements accurately if you are to create successful, satisfying patchwork. Many experienced needleworkers are able to do this by eye but I have never developed the knack. Instead, I use my own method with straight pins. This approach can be annoyingly time consuming but it is unfailingly accurate.

Step 1: Aligning the Squares (or Any Other Shape)

Lay out your fabric elements face up as indicated in your plan. Choose two squares sitting next to each other and flip one over the other so they are lying face to face.

Push a straight pin through one end of the sewing line (which is visible on the back of each square) so it pierces the exact end of the sewing line on the facing piece.

Repeat this process at the other end of the line and then in the middle. Each time, the pinpoint should meet the sewing line in the same spot on the opposite piece. If the lines don't match up, poke around with the point of the pin until you find the right position. Take time to be exact now and you will be glad with the results later. Every fraction of an inch that a square is off register will be multiplied as you join other pieces.

Consult the layout in front of you often to make sure you are joining the right edges. This can be critical if you are working with printed fabrics.

Step 2: Pinning to Sew

This first procedure was necessary to align the patches but now you must make room for the stitching.

You should now have 3 straight pins sitting exactly in the middle of the sewing line on one side of a patchwork shape. When you are satisfied that the two pieces are accurately registered with each other, insert 3 more pins at right angles to the sewing lines, as shown in the drawing. Remove the first 3 pins but do this only after you have placed the second 3 in position, or you will lose the registration.

Using pins to align patchwork squares.

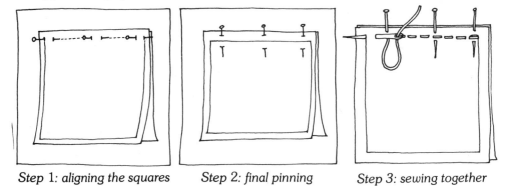

Step 1: aligning the squares   *Step 2: final pinning*   *Step 3: sewing together patchwork pieces*

Step 3: Sewing

When your first two patches are aligned and pinned, you are ready to sew. Thread your needle and make a knot at the end. Bring the point of the needle up at the exact beginning of the sewing line. Make one small running stitch forward along the line and one stitch back to secure the thread. Continue making small running stitches along the line until you reach the end. Secure the thread with another backstitch and bring the needle up for the final time through the end of the sewing line. Make a small knot and cut off the extra thread. Remove the pins, open the pair of patches, and put back in position in your layout. Continue to sew adjoining squares using this method. If you continue to keep your patchwork pieces in the correct position through each procedure, you will be sure not to make any sewing mistakes. It is very easy to become confused, especially if there is a lot of activity going on around you as you work.

DIAGONAL CHALLIS PILLOW

Both sides of the diagonal challis pillow are patchwork. The front side is made up of squares and triangles cut on the diagonal and the back contains four simple squares cut and sewn in traditional patchwork position. For this reason, if you are a newcomer to patchwork, you might complete the pillow back first and then go on to the front.

This pillow, as with most others in this collection, was made with sewing project leftovers, but it can be made easily with small amounts of challis from a yard goods shop. You will need ½ yard each of four contrasting prints. You might choose two prints in two different color combinations. Aside from color choices, also make sure that the textures created by the patterns sit well next to each other. To do this, place the fabrics side by side on a counter or shelf in the store and step back. The combination will have a busy look by nature of the prints but it should be a combination that is restful and pleasant. Challis is expensive, so choose carefully.

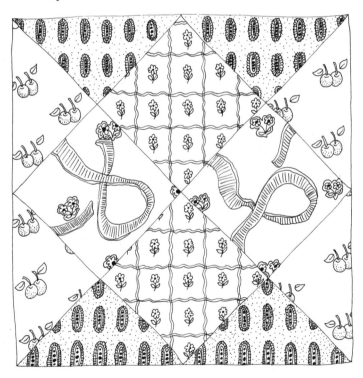

Materials Needed:

Finished size: 15 x 15 inches

For pillow front (as shown in illustration): ½ yard each of four printed pieces of cotton or wool challis

For pillow back (not shown): ½ yard each of two additional prints; or substitute solid-color fabric—one piece 15 x 15 inches (*plus seam allowance*)

Cardboard templates for pillow front: 5½-inch square; 5½ x 5½ x 7½-inch isosceles triangle

Cardboard template for pillow back: 7½-inch square

Soft pencil

Sharp scissors

Straight pins

Sewing needle and thread

Sewing machine (optional)

Iron

Pillow stuffing

Note: Beginners complete pillow back first, then proceed to pillow front.

To Make This Pillow:

1. For the *pillow back,* draw and cut out a cardboard template 7½ x 7½ inches.
2. Trace this template four times onto the *wrong side* of challis.
3. Cut out squares, leaving ¼-inch *seam allowance* on all sides of outlined edge.
4. Place all 4 challis squares in preferred position, face up.
5. Withdraw 2 adjoining squares from this arrangement. With *right sides* together, register, pin and stitch along one side as shown on page 123.
6. Open the joined pair, place again in layout and withdraw second pair. Join these along one seam, as in step 5.
7. Place both pairs, opened, face up, back in position. Flip one pair over the other so they are face to face.
8. Register, pin and stitch again, as shown on page 123. Open completed 4-patch fabric. Pillow back is now complete. Put aside and proceed with pillow front.

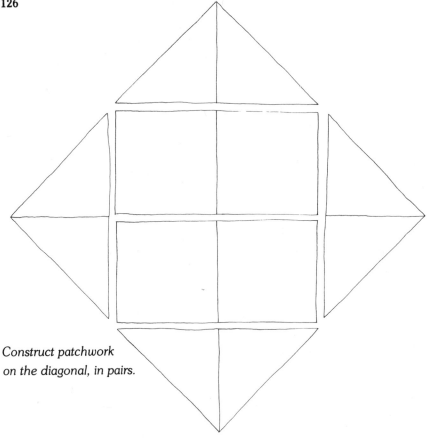

*Construct patchwork
on the diagonal, in pairs.*

Pillow Front:

1. Draw and cut two cardboard templates. Template 1 should measure 5½ inches square. Template 2 is an isosceles triangle with 5½-inch sides and 7½-inch base.
2. Trace template 1 two times on two different prints of challis on the *wrong side* of fabric (creating 4 squares).
3. Cut out traced squares, using sharp scissors and leaving ¼-inch seam allowance on all sides.
4. Trace template 2 four times on two different fabrics, creating 8 triangles.
5. Cut out traced triangles, using sharp scissors and leaving ¼-inch seam allowance on all sides.
6. Lay out all pieces in position, face up, on flat surface, according to layout shown on page 124.
7. Remove 2 squares from center of design, place face to face, align,

pin and stitch along one seam, as shown on page 123. Remove pins, open pair *right sides* out and replace in design.

Special note: Although I recommended stitching the central core and then adding the outside triangles, there are other orders that might make more sense to you when constructing this pillow top. The basic principle to keep in mind, when making patchwork, is to work with the smallest number of units possible at one time to keep the greatest possible manageability.

8. Remove 2 remaining squares and join in same manner. Replace *right sides* up in layout.
9. Join each pair of triangles along one seam in same way and return to layout. Be sure to join triangles at 5½-inch sides.
10. When all pairs are joined, press with hot iron and replace in layout.
11. Attach pairs of squares to each other by aligning, pinning and stitching.
12. Attach pairs of triangles to central panel using same method.
13. With hot iron, press all seams flat. Also press patchwork panel for pillow back.
14. Complete pillow in knife-edge construction shown on page 25 by joining front and back patchwork panels.

PATCHWORK PIE WEDGE

The pie-wedge pillow was done with the help of a commercial pattern. I had seen a number of interesting looking pillows in pattern books and finally I decided to give one a try.

The package came with two patterns and suggested variations for each. One was a patchwork pie-wedge pillow and the other a circular pillow with a gusset construction. For the circular gusset pillow, I used the suggested foam form and for the pie wedge I used my favored Dacron fiberfill. The gusset pillow was so harsh and unpleasant when complete that I put it in the garbage! The pie wedge is presented here with a few additional touches.

The pie-wedge pillow shown on the face of the pattern package was made of two alternating solid color fabrics. Instead, for greater richness, I used alternating paisley prints. When the pillow top was complete, I quilted lines next to each seam by machine (see page 178), and then did the final pillow construction. I also used the circular shape given for the back piece as a base for the appliqué vase of flowers on page 150 but instead I could have easily traced a circular pot or tray or other circular item the appropriate size.

Materials Needed:

Finished size: 15 inches across

Commercial pattern for pie-wedge pillow, or template made with compass, pencil, ruler and utility knife on 16 x 16-inch shirt cardboard

½ yard each of two contrasting fabrics (or amount indicated on pattern package), plus ½ yard of fabric for pillow back. (Add an additional ½ yard of contrasting fabric if you want pillow back to be same as pillow front.)

Needle and thread

Sewing machine (optional)

Pillow stuffing

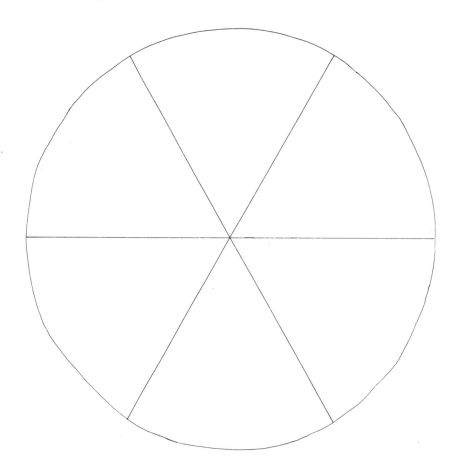

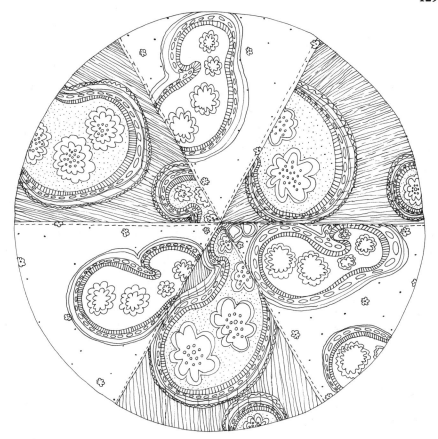

To Make This Pillow:

1. Pillow front: cut 3 wedges of each color by tracing cardboard template onto *wrong side* of fabric, as directed on pattern. Cut out, leaving ¼-inch seam allowance on all sides, or as directed on pattern.
2. Lay out all pieces in position, right sides up.
3. Join together, two at a time, using the method shown on page 123 to align, pin and stitch.
4. Continue with this procedure until all wedges are joined. Press all seams flat with hot iron.
5. Construct pillow according to instructions on page 25 for knife-edge pillow. Use a circular piece of fabric with a 14-inch diameter (*plus seam allowance*) for pillow back. (Or repeat directions above if you want pillow back and front to be the same.)

HEXAGON PILLOW

The hexagon pillow was made by Melanie Zwerling with fabric from worn-out clothing. The blouses she used were very full smocks, so she had more than enough fabric for her pillow. If you don't have scraps from retired clothing in the right colors and amounts, ½ yard each of three different prints plus ½ yard for the backing should be enough.

The hexagon pattern in patchwork is a traditional repeating design, but different patterns and color combinations can have radical effects on the finished pillow. The beauty of Melanie's pillow is in the soft, luxurious vision she created by choosing delicate, muted colors and soft, worn fabrics that reflect light in their fibers. If you are buying fabrics new rather than using worn materials, be sure to choose delicate cottons and wash them before assembling your pillow to dissolve any sizing.

To make a hexagon template, draw a circle with a compass on a piece of index board or shirt cardboard. Place the compass so its point lies on the circle's circumference and the pencil point touches the exact middle of the circle. (This is the hole left by the point of the compass). Carefully swing the pencil point from the middle of the circle so it intersects the circumference with a line, page 132. Place the compass point on this intersection and repeat the swing until you have marked a second intersection. Move the compass point to this intersection and make a third swing. Continue around the circle in this manner until you have marked six evenly spaced intersections. To make a perfect hexagon, connect these points with a pencil and ruler and then cut it out with a utility knife and metal-edged ruler.

Before you trace your hexagon template onto the fabric, make a color sketch on paper. There are so many combinations of pattern placement that it's best to work out the arrangement you want on paper first and cut out hexagon shapes according to what you have planned rather than leave the placement of colors to chance. Hexagons arranged in concentric circles can have a very strong, pleasing effect but they can also be very confusing if poorly arranged.

If you trace your hexagon on paper before you cut out your fabrics, you may devise an unusual arrangement or an arrangement that is better for your fabrics than the one used by Melanie.

Once you have an arrangement that you like, count the number of hexagons you will need in each color.

Trace and cut out the appropriate number and lay out your pieces as described earlier.

Sewing hexagons requires a different approach from stitching together squares because of the many sides of the hexagon. Begin in the center of your arrangement and add hexagons one at a time, working in a circular fashion.

Begin by sewing one hexagon of ring 1 to the central hexagon. Each new hexagon in ring 1 will be sewn in two places. It will be stitched to the central hexagon and also to the hexagon right next to it. You will have to ease each addition into position and use straight pins (see page 123) to help align the edges and corners. Follow the chart until you have completed ring 1.

Begin ring 2 by sewing the first hexagon in it to the edge of one hexagon in the previous ring. This first hexagon (and the first in every new ring) will be attached to the previous ring in only one place. The second hexagon in the ring will be attached in three places, the third in two places, and the fourth in three places. The number of sides that will be attached will be established by the preceding ring. Hexagons that fall on a corner will have two seams, hexagons that fall in the middle of a side will have three. If you look at the diagram, you will see why this happens.

Melanie stitched her hexagons together by hand, although it is possible to join them by machine. Her pillow is made of three rings around a central hexagon. When the hexagons were stitched in place, she quilted the pillow top according to the procedure outlined on page 182. Traditional quilting is done next to a patchwork shape. Instead, Melanie placed her quilt stitches into the seams of the hexagons. The result is a puffy, soft surface. She also added a delicate wooden button in the middle of the central hexagon as well as five short lines of quilting radiating out from the button. The finished pillow is a standard knife edge (see page 25), although the quilted surface makes it appear more intricate.

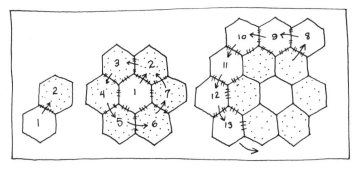

Joining hexagons

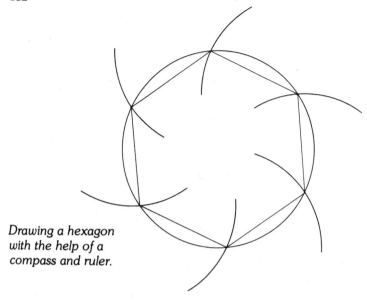

*Drawing a hexagon
with the help of a
compass and ruler.*

Materials Needed:

Finished size: 16 inches across

Cardboard hexagon template measuring 3 inches across (see accompanying instructions and diagram)
½ yard each of three different printed cotton fabrics
½ yard of fabric for pillow back
17 x 17-inch piece of Dacron quilt batting
17 x 17-inch piece of muslin (or other scrap material)
Small wooden button
Needle and thread
Sewing machine (optional)
Pillow stuffing

To Make This Pillow:

1. Draw a sketch of finished pillow on paper, indicating the placement of each print within layout. Use this as a guide for cutting hexagons in correct amounts of each and for sewing fabric together in the right sequence. You will need 37 hexagons in all.
2. Trace and cut the appropriate number of hexagons in each color on the *wrong side* of fabric as described on page 120. Be sure to leave ¼-inch seam allowance on all sides of each hexagon.

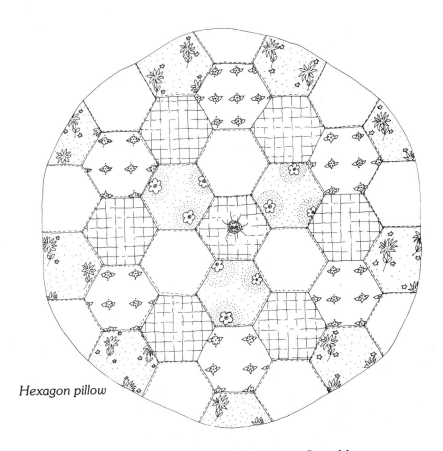

Hexagon pillow

3. Arrange hexagons in desired sequence on flat table.
4. Begin by joining one edge of one hexagon to an edge of the central hexagon, and work outward, as shown in diagram. For beginners, hand sewing is easier. Register hexagons with each other as described on page 122 and as shown on page 131.
5. Attach all hexagons in ring 1 and begin ring 2. Continue working outward until all hexagons are joined.
6. When patchwork pillow top is complete, press all seams flat with hot iron.
7. To quilt patchwork top, lay out on hard, flat surface from the bottom up: muslin, quilt batting and hexagon top, face up. Smooth all layers together.
8. Baste or pin three layers together, as described on page 179.
9. Make small quilt stitches in all seams, as shown on page 183, which will cause each hexagon to puff slightly.

10. When quilting is complete, remove basting stitches or pins. Stitch small button in middle of central hexagon. Trim batting and muslin flush with patchwork top.
11. Complete pillow in knife-edge construction, as described on page 25. Use a ready-made 16-inch circle (such as a dinner plate) to aid in construction. Outer ring of pillow top will become part of seam.

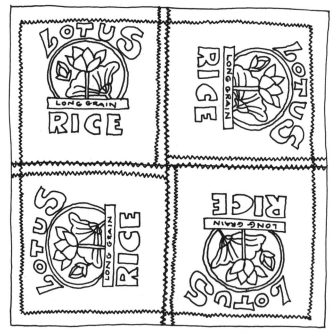

Completed patchwork rice-sack pillow

PATCHWORK RICE-SACK PILLOW

Most of the pillows in this book have been made with leftovers and scraps from sewing and needlework projects. Verena Mentzel's pillow of rice sacks is the only one I know of that has been made with materials that were actually plucked from the garbage!

Verena passed a pile of rice sacks outside of an import warehouse on Manhattan's Lower East Side and couldn't resist stopping. She rummaged through the pile and was able to unearth five or six clean white printed sacks. Tucking them under her arm, she continued down the street, knowing that she had just discovered real treasures. When she got home, she spread all of the sacks out on the floor and immediately decided to combine several together to make one large pillow. She found that she had an old down pillow that would make an ideal filling so she geared the finished pillow cover toward this.

When all the work was done, Verena was anxious to use her new pillow, yet she didn't want to stitch her down pillow permanently inside, so she made a lap-back construction as shown on page 32. When this was complete, she reversed the pillow and put in one more row of zigzag topstitching around the entire outside, about ¾ inch from the outside.

Materials Needed:

Finished size: approximately 16 x 16 inches

Four clean white muslin rice sacks with crudely printed design or lettering. These may be found through grocers who sell rice by the bag, but they may not be readily available. Feed and grain sacks of burlap, if clean, are also good; these are available through bulk animal-food suppliers.

Muslin—one piece the same size as patchwork made from rice sacks (*plus seam allowance*)

Needle and thread

Muslin, or fabric of your choice, 5 inches larger than rice-sack patchwork, for making removable pillow back, or the muslin the same size (*plus seam allowance*) as patchwork top for standard knife-edge pillow

Sewing machine with zigzag stitch (optional)

Ready-made pillow, same size as finished pillow top, or pillow stuffing for knife-edge construction

To Make This Pillow:

1. Lay sacks out in desired arrangement and join to each other two at a time, as shown in diagram and as described in patchwork section on page 120.
2. When all sacks are joined, press seams flat with hot iron.
3. With machine zigzag stitch set for *fine*, put in horizontal and vertical row of stitching on top of the two central seams, as shown on the following page.
4. Place muslin (which is the same size or slightly larger than patchwork rice-sack top) on hard surface and smooth patchwork top, right side up, in place on top. Pin or baste together securely.

5. Add 4 more lines of machine zigzag stitching and a line of stitching around the outside edge, as shown in the drawing on page 134.
6. Add additional zigzag stitching around any large illustrative marking on rice sacks. This will add strength and visual dimension to loosely woven sacks.
7. For removable pillow cover: Create lap back using fabric that is at least 5 inches larger than completed rice-sack top, as shown on page 31, and join to rice-sack front as described on page 31 for knife-edge pillow. Finished top should be 3 inches larger in dimension than size of pillow to be inserted.
8. Turn completed pillow cover right side out and machine zigzag around all sides, approximately ¾ inch from the outside.

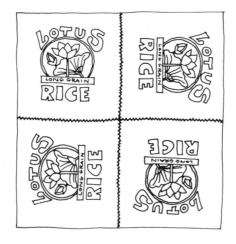

Step 3: machine zigzag stitching placed on top of two central seams.

RAINBOW MAT AND BOLSTER

Like many pillows in this book, the rainbow mat was inspired by a picture in a French craft magazine, *100 Idées*. The casual magazine browser might not recognize the similarities in the projects because the rainbow mat has taken on an identity of its own, yet I feel compelled to acknowledge the importance of good craft design and good photography.

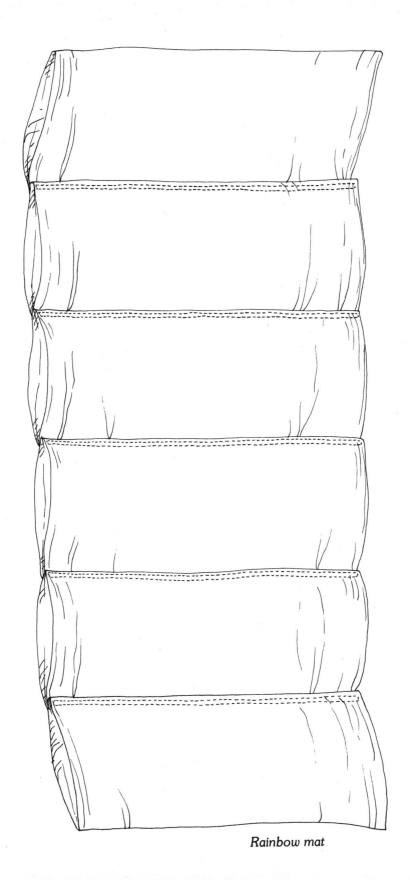

Rainbow mat

The rainbow mat and bolster were a house-warming gift for Stephen and Dorothy Globus, who wanted a spectacular-sized pillow for their spacious new loft. Dorothy and I had seen the rainbow quilt photograph together and we decided it would make a great floor cushion. The Globuses were delighted with their pillow furniture and found an ideal spot for it in a sunny south window. Recently, when Dorothy, Stephen and I were reminiscing about its development, I was reminded that I had reluctantly used polyester-blend fabric. Two years later, the mat and bolster looked fresh and new. The colors were bright and clear without any sign of fading.

Materials Needed for Mat:

Finished size: 90 x 34 inches

1 yard each of the following colors in cotton duck or polyester/cotton blend: red, orange, yellow, green, blue, violet. Be sure all colors are of the same intensity, so that when stitched together they will give a rainbow effect.
Needle, red sewing thread and sewing machine
Several large bags of Dacron fiberfill for pillow stuffing

To Make This Mat:

1. Cut a 35 x 35 inch piece from each piece of fabric.
2. Fold each square in half, *right sides* together, smooth and pin flat.
3. With sewing machine, straight stitch one short and one long side, as shown, to form a tube. Use red thread.
4. Clip corners of each tube, then turn right side out.
5. Push out all corners with fingers or blunt instrument and press each tube flat with iron.
6. Place tubes on floor in correct rainbow position as follows, with all tube openings on same side.
7. Place red tube (number 1) so it overlaps orange tube (number 2) slightly, about 1 inch.
8. Use straight pins to hold edges firmly in place and sew together with a double row of machine straight stitching.
9. Place joined red and orange tubes back in floor position and withdraw yellow and green tubes (numbers 3 and 4).
10. Place yellow tube so it overlaps green tube by 1 inch, pin and stitch.

11. Join blue and violet tubes (5 and 6) in the same way.
12. When all 3 pairs are joined, place back in correct rainbow position.
13. Join the pairs to each other as if they were single units, using same overlap and pin method.
14. When all tubes are joined, stuff them one at a time with Dacron fiberfill until each is firm but not bulging. Use your hand to distribute filling evenly.
15. Turn in all remaining raw edges, pin, and stitch shut with small hand stitches.

| Red |
| Orange |
| Yellow |
| Green |
| Blue |
| Violet |

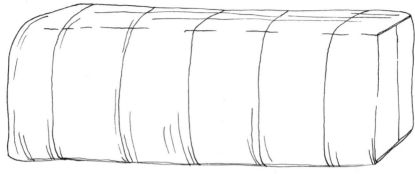

Rainbow bolster

Materials Needed for Bolster:

Finished size: 42 x 30 inches

Leftovers from the rainbow mat in colors described in previous project.
  Each piece should measure 7½ x 30½ inches
Needle, red sewing thread and sewing machine
Pillow stuffing

To Make This Bolster:

1. Lay out each color in correct rainbow position: red, orange, yellow, green, blue, violet.
2. Join long edges together with machine straight stitch, using method described on page 120 for patchwork.
3. When patchwork fabric is complete, press all seams flat with iron.
4. Pin patchwork piece in half lengthwise, right sides together. Pin securely and stitch down long edge, leaving an opening in center for filling pillow later.
5. Stitch each end closed ¼ inch from edge for *seam allowance.*
6. Following directions on page 27 for modified box pillow, stitch ½-inch diagonals into each corner.
7. Turn pillow right side out, stuff with Dacron fiberfill and hand stitch seam closed.

TURKISH BOLSTER

Once the Turkish pillow was complete (see page 35) I wanted to make a bolster to accompany it. I had already purchased a good-quality Dacron pillow form on sale in the pillow section of a department store, which would be ideal. It was 16 inches long and 19 inches in diameter. Since I was working with a prepared form, I was determined to keep the construction as simple as possible. In my search for design ideas, the pillow that caught my attention was a small eyelet-covered bolster that was wrapped and tied like a party favor.

Turkish bolster

Materials Needed:

Finished size: 16-inch-long cylinder

14 x 20-inch (*plus seam allowance*) piece of printed cotton fabric
Two 8 x 20-inch (*plus seam allowance*) pieces of solid-color cotton fabric
Two 36 x 4-inch pieces of the printed cotton fabric
Needle, thread and sewing machine
16-inch-long ready-made cylindrical pillow form

To Make This Bolster:

1. Construct pillow wrapper by joining 8 x 20-inch panels to each end of a 14 x 20-inch (*plus seam allowance*) piece of fabric, using the method described for patchwork on page 119.
2. Fold under raw edges at each end and hem with machine straight stitch.
3. Also turn under and machine hem one long edge of combined fabrics. Put aside.
4. Make ribbon ties by using 2 pieces of fabric 36 inches long by 4 inches wide. Fold each piece in half lengthwise, *right sides* together. Press flat with iron and pin securely.
5. Machine straight stitch across one end and down the length of each strip, as shown. Use a pencil and yardstick to mark stitch line before stitching, if desired.
6. Clip corners and reverse each strip by gently pulling fabric through remaining open end. Attach a large safety pin to one end of strip as an aid.
7. Press flat each reversed strip, fold in open end of each and hand stitch closed. Put aside.
8. To cover pillow form, place patchwork fabric, face down, on hard, flat surface. Place bolster form in the center of this, lining up the edges of the bolster with the edges of the central panel.
9. Wrap the unbound edge of the fabric firmly around the form and baste it to the form itself.
10. Wrap bound edge of fabric around form from the other side, covering the basted raw edge. Pin the bound edge firmly and stitch in place along entire edge with small hand stitches. Use a color thread that blends well with the fabric being used.
11. Gently gather the fabric at each end of bolster form and tie them close to the form itself with bows made from fabric ribbon described earlier.

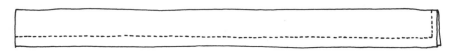

Stitching ribbon ties from a length of fabric

 **EIGHT**

Appliqué

APPLIQUÉ TECHNIQUES

Appliqué is the technique of placing one fabric on top of another and sewing it permanently in place. The process is always the same: cut, hem, place in position and sew down.

Traditional medium-weave cottons like calico, gingham, and muslin make delightful appliqué materials because they are so pleasant to look at and are available in such a wide variety of colors and prints. Appliqué pillow tops made of these materials are easy to make and are a pleasure to live with. The vase of flowers on page 150 and rabbit on page 153 were made with delicate cottons. Beware of fabrics that are mostly synthetic fiber. They are hard to manipulate and do not wear well.

Most fabrics used for appliqué require hemming as part of the procedure, but you can eliminate this if you choose felt as your material or substitute machine zigzagging instead of hand or machine straight stitching. Of course, the final result will be different. The shortcut approach generally produces shortcut results. There is still nothing as lovely as delicate hand stitching. The appliqué pillows in this section, with the exception of Edie Twining's designs, were all done with hand stitching.

TRADITIONAL APPLIQUÉ

Making a Template

To make an appliqué pillow with a pictorial shape of printed cotton fabric, such as the rabbit pillow, you will need to make a template, or pattern, to transfer the design. A template is especially useful if you intend to repeat the shape, as I did when making the flowers for the appliqué flower vase.

Using artwork from this book, from another source or of your own design, place a sheet of carbon paper between your drawing and a sheet of shirt cardboard, index card or blotter paper. (Tape several pieces of cardboard together, if necessary, when tracing large drawings.) To make the job easier, place the original on cardboard and tape down one edge. Slip the carbon, face down, between them. Trace over the lines of the original with a firm pencil line. Check to see that the lines have been transferred before separating the original and the cardboard. Finally, cut out the cardboard shape along the lines.

Using the Template

Place the template *right side up* on the *right side* of the fabric which, in preparation, has been pressed flat with an iron. Securing the template with one hand, trace around it with a medium pencil or chalk so the outline is visible on the fabric.

Using a template

Cutting the Appliqué Shape

Cut the appliqué shape out ¼ inch from the traced line. It is best to use scissors with at least 4-inch-long sharp straight blades for an even, clean cut. The extra ¼ inch all around is the hem allowance and if it is rough and frayed it will be difficult to handle.

Hemming

With the fabric right side up and the tracing facing you, use your thumb and index finger to fold under the hem allowance. Your fold should just barely include the tracing line. To do this correctly, fold away from you.

If you are working with shapes that have square corners, clip away the fabric diagonally across these corners for easy and clean hemming. If the appliqué shape is rounded, snip notches in the curves right up to the seam line (but not through!) for easy and accurate folding.

Use a running stitch with the knot on the top of the shape for easy removal later, and baste the edges under as you fold.

Special note: You may also use pins to hold your appliqué hems temporarily in place. Many people find the standard basting method painfully slow. These people are generally experienced enough to have developed some amount of control of the fabric they are working with. If you are a newcomer to appliqué, I suggest you stick to the full basting approach. It may be slightly slow but it allows one more control. I, for one, have never outgrown this method. You will need to use pins to hold your appliqué in place while you do final sewing.

Pressing

Steam all your edges under by applying the iron to the wrong side of the shape. This will make it more secure for permanent sewing. If your appliqué is stuck with pins rather than basted, place a cloth between the shape and the iron before you press.

Pinning in Position

Appliqué shapes tend to slip as they are being sewn down, and often you won't realize this until you have completed your painstaking stitches. To avoid this disaster, pin all shapes in exact position on the fabric background before you begin to do any final sewing. If your appliqué shape is large, use at least 3 pins to hold it securely. Wherever possible, place the pins in the interior of the shape to keep them from jabbing you. If the appliqué shape is small, consider basting it in place or hold the shape with your thumb as you stitch. Be sure to check the placement as you work to correct any movement. If your design contains elements that overlap each other, such as the appliqué flower vase, pin everything in position exactly as it will be in the final arrangement from the bottom up. You might even consider basting everything in position before doing your final stitching. If your design is simple and you have merely pinned the edges under in your preliminary hemming, reinsert some of the pins so they tack the appliqué to the base fabric.

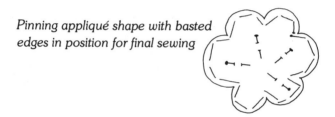

Pinning appliqué shape with basted edges in position for final sewing

Sewing in Place

All of the pinning and basting you have done so far has been meant to make the final sewing easy and relaxing. You should now be able to settle back into a comfortable chair and concentrate on making even, graceful stitches.

If you are stitching down traditional appliqué shapes, choose a running stitch, hem stitch or buttonhole stitch that will be visible on the surface of

The running stitch   *The hem stitch*   *The buttonhole stitch*

the finished appliqué. If you are experimenting with unusual forms of appliqué such as the lace lady or yo-yo fish you may want to make your stitches so they are as inconspicuous as possible. Experiment with scraps of fabric to see what you enjoy.

Thread

Choose your thread according to what you think is appropriate. If you want your stitching to contribute significantly to the finished appearance of your appliqué, choose brightly colored, multi-strand floss. Separate the strands for a more delicate appearance. If you want your stitches to be utilitarian rather than visual, choose a strong cotton thread such as bel-waxed or quilting thread. These threads resist most tangles and are easy to use.

For specifics on embroidery stitching, turn to page 44.

MACHINE APPLIQUÉ

Appliqué may also be done by machine, although machine-stitched pieces are often quite different in feeling from those done by hand. Machine stitching is informal, offering the advantages of strength and speed.

Straight Stitching

Use a machine straight stitch to appliqué large, simple shapes that have been pinned or basted to a backing fabric. Edie Twining used this method to make her whimsical family portrait.

Zigzag or Satin Stitching

If you have a reliable sewing machine, you may use this to zigzag shapes in place. Machines that will not satin stitch smoothly and consistently produce stitching that is unpleasant to look at and lacking in durability.

If your machine does work well, make sure your stitches have a good grip on the edges of the appliqué shape or it will separate from its base later. Try to keep at least three-quarters of the stitch on the appliqué shape. Or work with the technique used by Edie Twining. Place your machine zigzag stitches ¼ inch from the outside edge of the shape and when the stitching is complete, cut away the excess fabric from the outside. If you use this last method of machine appliqué you do not have to hem the appliqué shapes.

EXPERIMENTAL APPLIQUÉ

Anything that can be stitched to the surface of fabric should be considered for appliqué—from ribbon and old pieces of lace and crochet to old, decorative handkerchiefs, fabric flowers, buttons and beads. Consider comfort and durability when assembling materials for pillow stitchery. Large, sharp buttons or beads do not make for comfort, while simple, flat ones can be very workable.

Cotton ribbons make wonderful appliqués because they are so colorful and, as a bonus, need no hemming. Assemble ribbons carefully with an eye toward compatability. A mass of well-chosen ribbons can look very striking together (see Dorothy Globus's ribbon pillow on page 159), but those grabbed at random can be very discordant. Choose a few simple ribbons to decorate a flowered or gingham pillow top for a quick, informal pillow.

Old lace and pieces of crochet make dazzling appliqué material. Odd pieces from unfinished projects can be found at garage sales, thrift shops—and perhaps in your own attic. Doily making went out of style years ago, but we can use the remnants of this once popular hobby to create delicate, feminine pillows without spending hours stitching.

Use small, flat pictorial buttons such as ducks, fish, hearts or flowers as an added touch to your lace compositions or create an entire pillow picture by stitching down a mass of assorted mother-of-pearl buttons in simple shapes. These buttons, expensive to buy new by the half-dozen at your local variety store, turn up frequently by the jarful in thrift shops, antique shops and garage sales.

A pillow top decorated with many buttons will be very heavy, so be sure to choose a strong fabric for the pillow back.

YO-YOs

Yo-yos are decorative flower forms made from circles of cotton fabric that have been hemmed and drawn into a rosette shape. Yo-yo coverlets made from leftover scraps often appear in antique shops. A stitcher would fashion 40 or 50 and assemble them into a decorative (but unfortunately not warm) bed cover. Yo-yos are easy to make, particularly while traveling, because they require such small amounts of material. They are great stitched to themselves with a piece of muslin behind as a pillow cover. Or, do as I have done with my fish pillow on page 156. Turn them into a decorative element within a pillow.

To make a yo-yo, first make a template. On cardboard, draw a circle at least twice the size you want the finished flower to be and cut it out. Large tin cans make great ready-to-use templates (although cardboard makes a better template for traveling).

Trace the circular shape onto the *wrong side* of the fabric. Cut out the fabric ¼ inch outside the line. Turn in the edges of the circular shape right up to the line, making sure the hem falls over the *wrong side* of the fabric. Use a short running stitch to sew into the seam allowance ⅛ inch from the edge, all the way around. Make your stitches continuous, with no backstitches. The yo-yo is formed when you pull on the thread. This will force the edges of the circle together and leave a hole in the center. Use strong thread such as quilting thread or regular sewing thread doubled since the thread will have to support the tension of the fabric. When you begin stitching, bring the needle up from the underside so the knot will be hidden when the yo-yo is used. Stitch around the perimeter as evenly as possible and then pull smoothly to draw the circle into a yo-yo. Arrange the folds evenly and fasten with a few backstitches. Flatten the yo-yo and press with a damp cloth and warm iron.

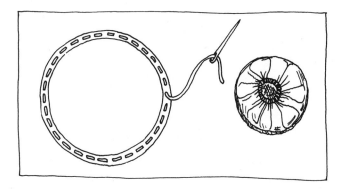

Yo-yos

APPLIQUÉ VASE OF FLOWERS

The appliqué vase of flowers was a pillow that I prepared at home and then stitched during the evenings while visiting in the country.

It is straightforward, traditional appliqué and the materials were assembled from the scrap bag.

Appliqué vase of flowers

Materials Needed:

Finished size: 15 inches across

15-inch circular template (dinner plate, tin tray or other ready-made circle)

Drawing of vase of flowers enlarged to appropriate size

15 x 15 inch sheet of lightweight cardboard (or several smaller pieces of shirt cardboard) for flower and vase templates

Cut the following amounts of cotton fabric (*plus seam allowance*):

   4 x 4-inch piece for each flower
   2 x 5-inch piece for each stem
   2 x 3-inch piece for each leaf
   5 x 6-inch piece for vase
   8 x 3½-inch piece for tablecloth

Two pieces of 16 x 16-inch cotton fabric or pillow front and back

16 x 16-inch piece of Dacron quilt batting

16 x 16-inch piece of muslin

Small needle and white quilting thread (or standard sewing thread)

Pillow stuffing

Outline of shapes for appliqué vase of flowers

To Make This Pillow:

1. Trace 15-inch circle on the *right side* of cotton fabric that measures at least 16 x 16 inches. Trace a second circle the same size on another piece of fabric for the pillow back. Cut out, leaving ¼-inch seam allowance on all sides.
2. Enlarge drawing on grid to appropriate size, as directed on page 16.
3. Make templates by using carbon paper to transfer all shapes onto shirt cardboard. Cut out each shape separately with sharp scissors.
4. Use templates as described on page 144. Trace each flower onto the *right side* of 4 x 4 inch fabric and the flower centers onto 1½ x 1½ inch pieces of fabric. Trace stem templates onto 2 x 5 inch fabric and leaf templates onto 2 x 3 inch fabric. Trace tablecloth template onto 8 x 3½ inch fabric.
5. Cut all traced shapes ¼ inch outside pencil line and hem under all edges. Press all pieces with iron.
6. Pin (and baste if necessary) all circular hemmed appliqué shapes in position on the fabric that is to be the pillow front. Be sure appliqué shapes are layered in correct position for final sewing: the vase should sit on top of tablecloth, the flowers should sit on top of stems, the stems should cover the ends of the leaves as well as be tucked into vase on the bottom.
7. When appliqué shapes are firmly pinned or basted in correct position, stitch them in place with tiny hand stitches such as a hem stitch or stem stitch. Use white quilting thread, if possible, or standard sewing thread.
8. When final sewing is complete, remove pins or basting stitches.
9. Quilt appliqué top as directed on page 183. Place same size circular piece of muslin on hard surface, then same size Dacron quilt batting and, finally, on top, appliqué top, face up.
10. Pin or baste three layers firmly together.
11. Place small quilting stitches around each appliqué shape. Add a French knot and several satin stitches inside both circular flower centers.
12. Complete pillow according to instructions for knife-edge pillow (page 25), using circle traced onto 16 x 16 inch fabric for pillow back.

RABBIT RIBBON PILLOW

The rabbit ribbon pillow was made by Brenda Murphy to match her blue and white bedroom. The pillow has a delicate, soft quality that was created by careful planning and choice of materials as well as patient hand stitching.

Brenda first chose her backing fabric, a delightful blue and white check that might well be men's shirting. The appliqué rabbit is a light and dark blue gingham. Both fabrics were left over from previous sewing projects.

The appliqué elements in this pillow are so charmingly simple and easy to work with that they deserve further consideration by you as a pillow maker. Beautiful fabric and well-chosen trimmings together make quick but wonderfully decorative pillows. The simple appliqué rabbit may be appliquéd in multiples on a carefully chosen background. Just trace the template several times and choose an appropriately larger base fabric. Or consider the basic rabbit and ribbon pillow in other color combinations such as yellow and white or shades of lavender. Brenda made the original pillow to suit her tastes and needs. Why not try to adapt it to your own ideas?

Materials Needed:

Finished size: 12 x 12 inches

Cardboard template made from rabbit drawing shown on page 153, which has been enlarged to the appropriate size

Two pieces of cotton fabric 12 x 12 inches (*plus seam allowance*) for pillow front and back

7 x 7-inch piece of contrasting fabric for rabbit appliqué

One 50-inch length of grosgrain ribbon

One 50-inch length of flower-embroidered ribbon

One 50-inch length of delicate rickrack

Small skein of cotton embroidery floss in appropriate color

Embroidery needle

Embroidery hoop (optional)

Sewing machine (optional)

Pillow stuffing

To Make This Pillow:

1. Enlarge rabbit drawing on page 153 to appropriate size, as described on page 16.
2. Transfer enlargement to shirt cardboard using carbon paper and cut out along outline using sharp scissors.
3. Trace template onto *right side* of fabric, using soft pencil or dressmaker's chalk.
4. With sharp scissors, cut out rabbit shape, leaving ¼-inch seam allowance on all sides. Make small clips in all curved edges of rabbit's outline up to (but not through) traced outline.
5. Fold under and baste all edges. Press with iron.
6. Pin basted rabbit in center of 12 x 12 inch fabric to be pillow front.
7. Stitch rabbit permanently in place with neat buttonhole stitches (page 48) using the embroidery floss.
8. Pin ribbon and rickrack trim in position, running in one direction only, as shown. Stitch in position with small hand stitches and standard sewing thread or by machine.
9. Pin ribbon and rickrack trim running in perpendicular position, so they overlap trimming already in place. Stitch down.
10. Complete pillow in knife-edge construction as described on page 25.

YO-YO FISH PILLOW

The yo-yo fish pillow was inspired by a beautifully sewn fish Christmas ornament. The ornament itself was so tiny that it was hard to imagine how anyone had been able to create such miniature yo-yos. On the other hand, I was fascinated by the idea of using the more common size of yo-yo in a larger fish pillow.

Materials Needed:

Finished size: approximately 15 x 9 inches

Cardboard template made from fish outline, enlarged to appropriate size (approximately 15 x 9 inches)
Cardboard template for 3¼-inch circle
Two pieces of solid-color cotton fabric, each measuring 12 x 17 inches (*plus seam allowance*) for front and back of fish body
½ yard each of two printed cotton fabrics for yo-yos
One ball each of four colors of pearl cotton
Embroidery needle
Sewing machine (optional)
Pillow stuffing

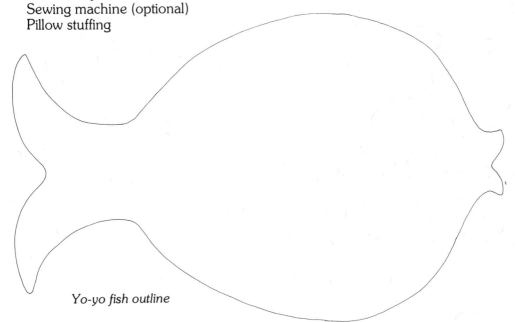

Yo-yo fish outline

Yo-yo fish

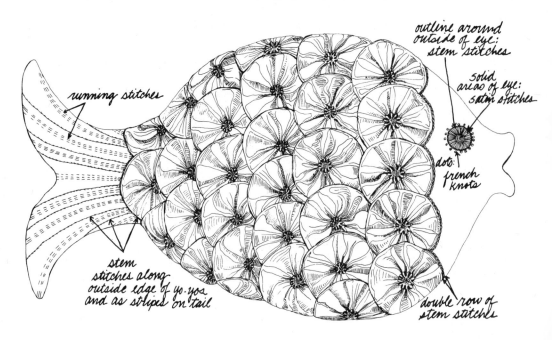

outline around
outside of eye:
stem stitches

solid
areas of eye:
satin stitches

running stitches

dots:
french
knots

stem
stitches along
outside edge of yo-yos
and as striped on tail

double row of
stem stitches

To Make This Pillow:

1. Using grid method, enlarge outline of fish to appropriate size (approximately 15 x 9 inches) according to instructions on page 16.
2. Using carbon paper, transfer enlargement to cardboard to make template. Cut out along traced edge.
3. Trace template onto wrong side of fabric for front and back of fish. For pillow back, flip template over so pieces will match when being constructed. Carefully mark front of each piece, as they can be easily confused later. Set aside. Transfer locations for embroidery, using carbon paper, to right side of fish body, if desired.
4. Draw a 3¼-inch circle on cardboard or trace a circle from a tin can or other circular object.
5. Cut out circle along traced line.
6. Using the circular template as described on page 149, trace 36 circles onto the *wrong side* of two different printed cottons. You will need 20 circles of one color and 16 of the other.
7. Cut out all circles ¼ inch from traced line and draw into yo-yos, as shown on page 149.

8. Beginning at fish's tail, pin yo-yos in position on fish shape. The first row should contain the yo-yos that have been cut in larger quantity, as directed in step 6.
9. When all yo-yos are in position, stitch down with tiny hand stitches using standard sewing thread. You will need to stitch only one side of yo-yos in each row; the other side will be overlapped by the following row. The last row of yo-yos (nearest the fish's face) will be sitting on top, as shown, and need stitching on all sides.
10. When yo-yos are sewn in place, add embroidery using simple straight stitches on page 51, stem stitches on page 52, and French knots, shown on page 49.
11. Pin completed fish front to fish back, *right sides* together, and stitch around outside ¼ inch in from edge as directed for knife-edge construction (page 25). Clip into (but not through) curved seams of tail and mouth before reversing. Be sure to leave a 3-inch opening along bottom edge of fish for reversing and stuffing.

RIBBON PILLOWS

Dorothy Globus has always been excited by the dazzling selection of ribbons at Hyman Hendler, ribbon and trimmings mecca in New York City, but usually has to satisfy herself with purchasing single ribbons to tie back her hair. Finally, when she and her husband Stephen moved into their spacious new loft, she had just the excuse she needed. I gladly accompanied her on a buying trip to Hendler's for a selection of ribbons to be stitched together into pillows.

For anyone who likes sewing, needlecraft or just pretty things, walking into this store can be both exhilarating and frustrating. Dorothy and I spent our first fifteen minutes passionately swooning over striped, flowered, plaid and dotted ribbons. We suggested possible combinations to each other, agreeing that each idea sounded better than the one before. We pointed out ribbons to each other, superimposed those we dared touch and after a half-hour we had overwhelmed each other with expensive ideas for pillows. The ribbons were getting the best of us.

Realizing the obstacles, Dorothy and I decided on a more systematic approach: Dorothy would choose a color combination and we would then assemble appropriate ribbons. Making the first choice was probably the hardest because there were so many enticing combinations, but in the end Dorothy considered the furniture and needlework she already owned and the colors she would enjoy looking at once outside the stimulating store environment. Brown, beige, navy and white was the color scheme that filled all of Dorothy's requirements, and the number of ribbons available in these colors was still staggering!

The next phase of selection was to focus on a few favorite ribbons. We had no trouble doing this, as some dotted and striped grosgrain ribbons had been catching our attention from the start. We grouped together three or four of our favorites but decided that for a really exciting ribbon composition, we would need three or four more choices in addition.

After some arranging, adding and substituting, we had arrived at a selection of 12 ribbons, from an inch to an inch and a half wide, which Dorothy purchased in 1-yard lengths. She also bought one yard of a striped 2-inch-wide grosgrain ribbon as a gusset for one of the pillows.

Pillow 1: Ribbon-Gusset Pillow

Finished size: 18 x 11 inches with 1½-inch gusset

Materials Needed:

One piece of muslin 18 x 11 inches (*plus seam allowance*)
One piece of velveteen 18 x 11 inches (*plus seam allowance*)
19 inches of each of 10 different grosgrain ribbons in widths varying from 1 to 1½ inches
60 inches of 2-inch-wide grosgrain ribbon for pillow gusset
Sewing machine
Pillow stuffing

To Make Ribbon-Gusset Pillow:

1. Place ribbons in pleasing arrangement on flat surface. Remove ribbon from one edge of arrangement and pin it in place on one edge of muslin, leaving a ¼-inch seam allowance along length of ribbon.
2. Sew in place with small running stitches (page 44) in a color that blends with ribbon.
3. Remove next ribbon in layout, pin in place abutting (but not overlapping) first ribbon, and stitch in place.
4. Continue pinning and stitching ribbons in place one at a time until all are sewn down. Trim all ends flush with muslin.
5. Add ribbon gusset by pinning 2-inch-wide grosgrain ribbon *right sides* together with completed ribbon top, as described under box pillow on page 30. Ease ribbon around all corners.

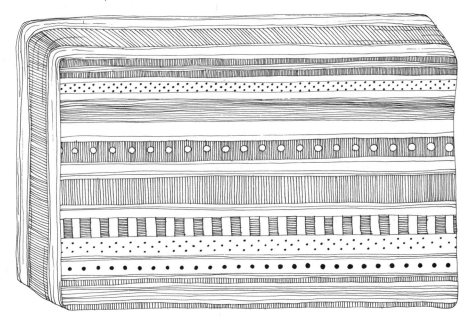

Ribbon-gusset pillow

6. Use sewing machine to stitch pinned edge of ribbon to pillow front.
7. Pin velveteen fabric for pillow back *right sides* together with other edge of ribbon gusset, again easing ribbon around all corners.
8. Stitch ribbon and velveteen together, leaving approximately 3 inches open along one side for reversing and stuffing pillow.
9. Reverse pillow, clip corners up to (but not through) stitching to ease tension, stuff and stitch closed by hand.

Pillow 2: Knife-edge Ribbon Pillow

Finished size: 14 x 8½ inches

Materials Needed:

One piece of muslin 14 x 8½ inches (*plus seam allowance*)
One piece of velveteen 14 x 8½ inches (*plus seam allowance*)
Two ribbons 18 inches long
Seven ribbons 9 inches long, all in widths varying from 1 to 1½ inches
Sewing machine (optional)
Pillow stuffing

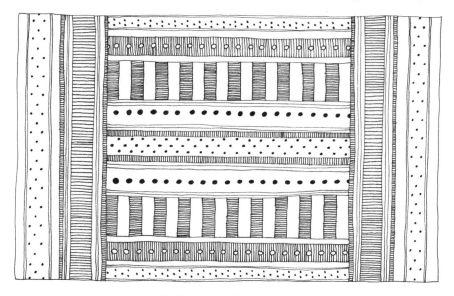

Knife-edge ribbon pillow

To Make Knife-edge Ribbon Pillow:

1. Place all ribbons in a pleasing arrangement on flat surface. Remove ribbons one at a time from arrangement, pin securely in position on muslin and stitch down with small running stitches using sewing thread that blends with ribbon (see step 2 in previous project).
2. Continue placing and stitching ribbons until all are in place so each new addition abuts but does not overlap adjoining ribbon.
3. Complete pillow in knife-edge construction (page 25) using velveteen as pillow back.

LACE APPLIQUÉ PILLOWS

Most of the pieces of lace for these pillows came from a bag found tucked away in an attic drawer. The bag contained crochet pieces from several unfinished projects. I was so charmed by them as I pulled them out of the bag that I immediately began to think of ways to use them. If you aren't so lucky as to have an old family attic or basement to rummage around in, don't despair. Keep your eyes open for retired needlewook in thrift shops, antique stores, flea markets and garage sales. Usually you will find a basket or box hidden in a corner filled with assorted pieces of lace. Except by a few collectors of the lace itself, these pieces are passed over by the average browser. As a result, this delicate needlework, which took hours to create, sits gathering dust with modest price tags attached to it. You might even ask around among your friends and acquaintances. Someone may have just such a collection of old half-started needlework projects that they would be only too delighted to get rid of.

LACE LANDSCAPE

After the initial excitement of discovery had subsided, I spent two or three hours arranging and rearranging the lace pieces in combination with other potential materials. More time was spent in the selection and arrangement of colors, textures and fabrics than was spent in the actual sewing.

Materials Needed:

Finished size: approximately 27 x 17 inches (though size may differ depending on amount of lace scraps on hand)

Special note: Because the lace landscape and the lace lady were both made from scraps of lace and crochet (the acquisition of which was described in the previous section), it will be almost impossible for you to duplicate these pillows exactly. Do not despair. Keep your eyes open at garage sales and flea markets, collect your own lace scraps and create your own lace compositions using the same procedures I did.

Assorted lace and crochet scraps
Buttons
One piece of velveteen in appropriate size for pillow front plus additional piece (in same size) for pillow back
Fabric for patchwork borders, where desired (be sure to account for any patchwork additions when determining fabric size of pillow back)
Needle and thread
Sewing machine (optional)
Pillow stuffing

Lace landscape

To Make This Pillow:

1. On flat surface, arrange scraps into image of house, tree and pond (as shown in drawing).
2. Once you have a pleasing arrangment, pin all elements securely in place on velveteen backing fabric in color that contrasts with lace. Fabric should be large enough to accommodate lace arrangement *plus seam allowance.*
3. Stitch all elements in position using white sewing or quilting thread to make tiny stitches.
4. Add any buttons and running-stitch details using standard white sewing or quilting thread.
5. Add patchwork border as described on page 119.
6. Add ribbon or lace trimming over border by pinning in position and machine stitching.
7. Finish pillow in knife-edge construction (page 25) using fabric in same dimensions as finished pillow front plus ¼-inch seam allowance.

LACE LADY

Once I discovered the crochet lace scraps in the family attic I began to collect other odd pieces of white needlework. After a summer of yard sales, bazaars and antique shopping, I had acquired a large collection of odd shapes and sizes. I was sure I had the makings of some wonderful pillow decorations. I had already completed the lace landscape (see page 161) by laying lace out flat on a background fabric. Now I wanted to be more adventurous. I pulled out my various odd pieces and began to play around with them. Suddenly there appeared in front of me the vision of the lace lady.

Materials Needed:

Finished size: approximately 23 x 13½ inches

Assorted lace, crochet scraps, delicate handworked handkerchiefs, ribbons, buttons. (See special note on page 161.)

One piece of velveteen in appropriate size for pillow front, plus one additional piece (in same size) of velveteen or printed polished cotton for pillow back

Enough cotton fabric to make appliqué head, hands and feet of lace lady

Lace that measures four times the perimeter of completed pillow top to be stitched into pillow construction

Needle and thread

Sewing machine (optional)

Pillow stuffing

To Make This Pillow:

1. On a large piece of velveteen arrange laces and trimmings to form figure of lady. Gather lace and handkerchiefs with running stitches to create sleeves, a neckline and waist.
2. Use simple appliqué shapes to create a head, hands and feet out of cotton fabric. Cut and baste these as described on page 145 and include in lace composition.
3. Pin all elements in position on velveteen backing fabric. Be sure lace overlaps basted cotton appliqué shapes where necessary.
4. When all elements are pinned in final arrangement, sew in place with small stitches. Use standard sewing thread.

Lace lady

5. When sewing is complete, add embroidery details using pearl cotton. Draw flowers or other shapes on paper and transfer to surface of velveteen with dressmaker's carbon or draw directly on surface of velveteen, if preferred. Use simple straight stitches (page 51) and hem stitches as described on page 146.

6. Add lace ruffle around entire edge of completed appliqué top as described on page 33.

7. Finish pillow in knife-edge construction as described on page 25, using velveteen or heavy printed polished cotton cut to same size as pillow front (*plus seam allowance*). Do not include width of lace ruffle in measurement.

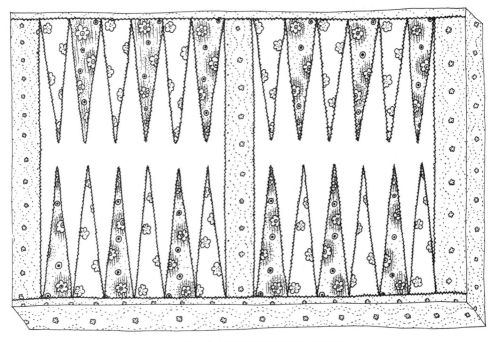

BACKGAMMON PILLOW

The backgammon pillow was made by Edie Twining, who has collected a wonderful assortment of fabrics and trimmings that she keeps in cubby-holes in her bedroom. Edie chooses fabrics from her collection as a painter would select tubes of paint. For her brush she has a nifty Elna sewing machine that makes consistent, tightly packed zigzag stitches.

Edie likes to select her materials, sit at her sewing machine with scissors and pins and improvise to create one-of-a-kind pillows. Her first back-gammon pillow was made this way, but it was so popular with friends and relatives that she went on to make several more as gifts, each slightly different.

Edie's backgammon pillow is a combination of appliqué and patch-work done with the sewing machine. Because she used zigzag satin stitches, which bind off raw edges of fabric, she was able to cut, place and stitch her appliqué shapes in place without doing any time-consum-ing hemming. If you have a sewing maching that will zigzag reliably without catching on itself, you'll have no trouble following Edie's proce-dure for the appliqué top. If you have a machine like mine, which would rather jam then stitch a long, even zigzag row, it is best to hem your backgammon points and machine straight stitch them in position accord-ing to traditional appliqué methods on page 147.

Materials Needed:

Finished size: 30 x 19 x 2 inches

Assortment of printed and solid-color fabrics in colors that blend well
    together: ½ yard of solid-color velveteen; 2½-yard pieces of printed
    cotton in coordinating colors (to be cut and appliquéd to velveteen
    bases); 2 yards of contrasting printed cotton for patchwork construc-
    tion and pillow back
12½ x 6-inch piece of cotton fabric for pocket (optional)
Sewing machine with reliable zigzag stitch. (This pillow may also be made
    with machine straight stitching or by hand—see step 3 of next section.)
Soft pencil and yardstick
30 x 19 x 2-inch foam form (available at sewing specialty shops)

To Make This Pillow:

1. Construct appliqué panels first by cutting velveteen into two 12 x 18 inch panels (*plus seam allowance*).
2. Cut fabric of two alternating colors or prints into 24 elongated tri-angles measuring 8½ inches high and 2 inches across. Use the diagram here as a guide for drafting a cardboard template and trace onto *right side* of fabric as described in section on appliqué (page 144).

3. For machine zigzag appliqué, cut out triangles' outline. For traditional appliqué, cut out triangles with ¼-inch seam allowance, hem and baste according to instructions in appliqué section.

4. Center and pin triangles in alternating colors to each 12 x 18 inch panel, as shown. Be sure to arrange them correctly and continue to check their placement until they are firmly pinned. Incorrect placement will interfere with playing the game.

5. When all triangles or backgammon "points" are smooth and pinned in position, stitch them in place with small, compact machine zigzag stitching, making sure stitches firmly grip both appliqué shapes and base fabric. Triangles that have been pinned with hems may be machine straight stitched in position or sewn by hand.

6. When appliqué is complete, cut three 2 x 18 inch and 2 x 30 inch strips of fabric from printed fabric intended as base for pillow. Use a pencil and ruler to draft these dimensions on cardboard for templates described earlier.

7. Also cut a 19 x 30 inch (*plus seam allowance*) piece from same fabric for pillow back. A 12½ x 6 inch piece may be cut for optional pocket.

8. Lay out all patchwork pieces of pillow top, including appliqué panels, in correct position, as shown.

9. Using method described on page 120 of the patchwork section, begin assembly with center pieces and work outward.

10. Use straight pins, as described on page 123, to register all increments as you work. Replace all pieces into layout, face up, as they are stitched, to avoid possible mistakes in assembly. Press pieces flat with iron.

11. When patchwork appliqué pillow top is complete, construct pillow boxing by joining 30 x 2 inch strips to the long sides and 18 x 2 inch strips to the short sides of completed top using method described on page 123 for aligning patchwork.

12. Register and pin corner seam allowances face to face and stitch up all 4 corners.

13. Add 12½ x 6 inch pocket to pillow back, if desired. Turn under one long side ½ inch and straight stitch down to form hem. Center this on center of pillow back, pin in place and machine zigzag 3 raw edges. Machine stitch strips of Velcro to top lip of pocket and corresponding spot on pillow back, if desired, before stitching pocket in place.

14. Add 19 x 30 inch pillow back by placing it face to face with completed pillow front and side panels. Use straight pins to register and attach pillow back to boxing strips around pillow top, using seam-allowance markings as guide.
15. Straight stitch in place around 3 sides. Remove pins, insert pillow form, pin the seam shut and sew closed with small hand stitches.

Backgammon pillow

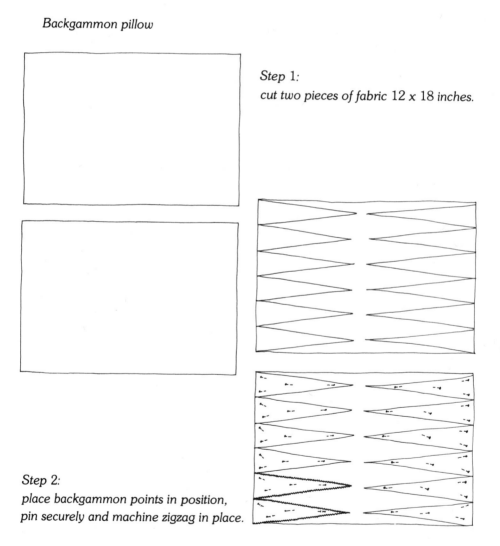

Step 1:
cut two pieces of fabric 12 x 18 inches.

Step 2:
place backgammon points in position,
pin securely and machine zigzag in place.

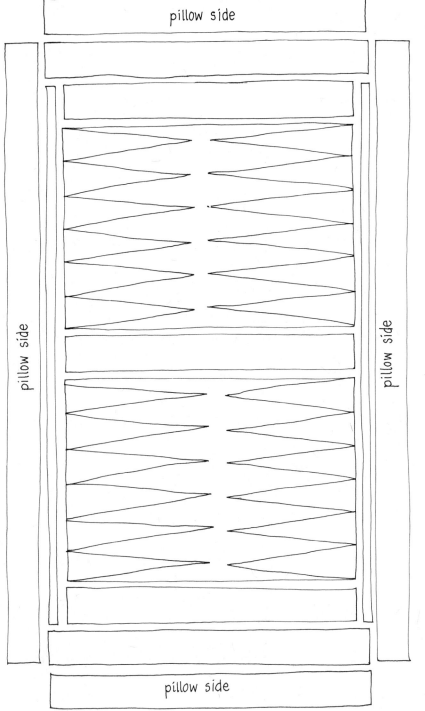

*Adding strips for backgammon border and patchwork pillow
sides as described on page 000*

APPLIQUÉ FAMILY

Edie Twining's oversize pillow is a whimsical family portrait. Edie has put her parents in the center of the pillow and has surrounded them with representations of her brother, her two sisters and their husbands, herself and the family dogs.

To devise her portraits, Edie used a surprising combination of materials—tweeds, plaids, Indian printed cottons, corduroys, denim and silk. All are stitched to a soft, loosely woven white base fabric, which is edged on top and bottom with red wide-wale corduroy. These fabrics might seem hopelessly unrelated when seen in a scrap bag, but Edie combined them in a way that makes them appear to be almost woven on the pillow's surface. The fabrics were chosen with great care to represent the tastes of each person. Mrs. Twining wears a striped silk dress and Mr. Twining is relaxing in green corduroy pants and a blue button-down shirt. They both sit on a black and white houndstooth couch. Edie's brother Alexander wears denim jeans and a plaid shirt while she has dressed herself in a loose Indian print blouse and pants. All portraits have white muslin faces on which Edie drew softly penciled features. She also used an assortment of upholstery trimmings, bought as remnants, in solids and tweeds, to put hair on the heads of everyone in the picture. Willie, the dog, is made of a random but somehow dog-shaped mass of silk threads while Sam, the Laborador retriever, is a distinctly dog-looking patch of black corduroy.

Rather than directly copy Edie's personal family portrait you will probably want to create a pillow that symbolizes your own family or group of friends. To do this read the introduction to this chapter for ideas on technique and begin to assemble materials.

Materials Needed:

Finished size: 18 x 24 inches

One piece of heavy, solid-color fabric—14 x 24 inches (*plus seam allowance*)

Two pieces of corduroy—each 2 x 24 inches (*plus seam allowance*)

Fabric for pillow back—18 x 24 inches (*plus seam allowance*)

14 x 24-inch lightweight cardboard or an assortment of smaller pieces of shirt cardboard for templates

Assortment of scrap fabrics in checks, plaids, prints and solids ranging in
    size from 6 x 6 inches downward. Small pieces of solid fabric for each
    face.
Yarn, string or other trimming for hair
Pencil or other implement for delineating faces
Needle and thread
Sewing machine (optional)
Pillow stuffing

Appliqué family

To Make This Pillow:

1. Join two corduroy strips to top and bottom of 14 x 24 inch panel as seen in photograph in the color section.
2. Enlarge drawing of family to appropriate size or create your own to size using a photograph or your own ideas.
3. Transfer drawing to cardboard as described on page 16 to create templates for each shape to be appliquéd, if desired. Or, for a more loose effect, draw basic shapes freehand directly on fabric with pencil.
4. Cut out all shapes ¼ inch from outline, turn under, hem and baste.
5. Arrange all appliqué shapes on surface of pillow top and pin in position.
6. Hand stitch or machine appliqué all edges with a small straight stitch.
7. Add hair to heads by hand stitching clumps of yarn, threads or tassels from upholstery trimming in position.
8. Using a pencil, draw simple facial details in position. If desired, transfer tracings of faces from the drawing in this book, using graphite carbon.
9. Finish pillow using knife-edge construction described on page 25.

SOCK PILLOWS

One day Dorothy Globus and I were browsing through our favorite French craft magazine, *100 Idées,* when we turned to a picture of assorted striped soccer socks—all child sized—that had been turned into a delightful wall hanging. We agreed that it was a great craft idea if brightly colored socks were part of your child's wardrobe. Then we turned the page and went on to something else.

Several weeks later Dorothy called me on the phone, full of excitement. Did I remember the sock wall hanging we had seen together? I did. She had bought 100 pairs of striped socks at 10 cents a pair and was planning to make a sock quilt! When I saw the socks I too became excited. These were no ordinary striped socks. They were circa 1945 knit socks in exquisite muted stripes. Dorothy spent the summer working on her quilt. She machine appliquéd the socks in place using a printed sheet for her base fabric. She lightly stuffed each sock through an open side she had left in the stitching and then closed each sock up by hand. Once this was complete, she finished off the quilt with an interlining and a backing fabric that coordinated with the print used for the quilt top. The results were extraordinary! Dorothy and her quilt appeared in the September '76 *House and Garden*.

When the quilt was complete there were socks left over. Dorothy went to work assembling them into incredible stuffed feet. First she stuffed the socks with Dacron fiberfill and tied off the tops with neat string bows. When this was done, she laid the stuffed socks out on the floor and began to experiment with arrangements. Using 20 socks, she was able to devise three completely different sock pillows. Two pillows appear to be dancing feet—one group dancing sideways, the other group dancing forward and back. The third pillow is a geometric arrangement of six pillows radiating from a central point. Aside from the shapes of the stuffed socks being so whimsical in themselves, the stripes are so varied and offbeat that they play a large part in the overall humor of the pillows.

The fourth sock pillow (third from left in the color picture in the color section) was made by me from some of Dorothy's leftovers. For a base fabric I used a green cloth table napkin that was 14 x 14 inches. I experimented with the arrangement of the socks and once I was satisfied with the placement, I pinned the socks in position, as I would with any traditional appliqué shape. I stitched the socks in place with a delicate hand hem stitch. When this was complete, I made small slits in the back of the green napkin in the center of each sock, being careful not to accidentally pierce a sock. It was easy to tell where to cut because the shape of each one was now delineated by the hem stitching. Using a crochet hook, I lightly stuffed each with Dacron fiberfill and then stitched up each hole. When filling the socks, I had to avoid being too generous with the stuffing because if the socks were too tightly packed, they would buckle the base fabric.

Materials Needed for Pillows 1–3:

Special note: You may not be able to locate exactly the same socks used in the projects shown here, but other decorative socks can be successfully substituted.

Sock pillows 1, 2 and 3 (all are shown in color section; but see further pages 174–175 for sock pillows 1 and 2):

20 socks in colors and patterns that blend well with each other
Pillow stuffing

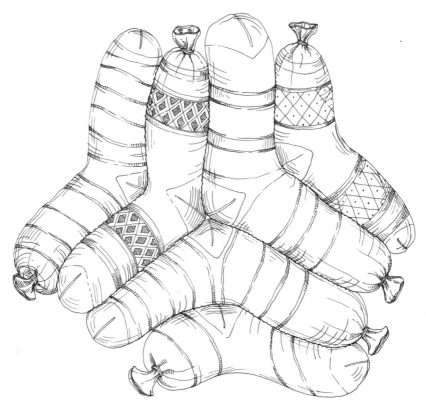

Sock pillow 1

To Make Pillows 1–3:

1. Stuff 20 socks with Dacron fiberfill. Next, close each sock with small running stitches approximately 1 inch from sock top, creating a sausage effect.
2. Assemble the socks into arrangements that best enhance their colors and patterns as shown in drawings above and photograph in color section. Arrange socks in groups of 6 or 7 if you wish to make three pillows, as shown.
3. When you have selected your final arrangements, stitch socks to each other, one at a time, with small running stitches placed down points where socks abut. Use standard sewing thread.
4. Continue adding socks in this manner until arrangement is complete.

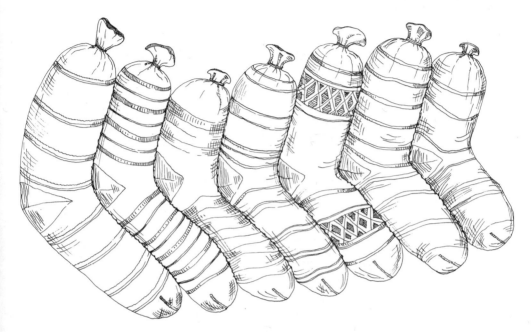

Sock pillow 2

Materials Needed for Pillow 4:

Sock pillow 4 (shown in color section and on page 176):

Four socks in colors and patterns that blend well with each other
14 x 14-inch (*plus seam allowance*) solid-color base fabric. (A cloth napkin is excellent.)
60-inch length of grosgrain ribbon
Cotton fabric in same measurements as completed sock top (including ribbon border)
Needle and thread
Sewing machine
Pillow stuffing

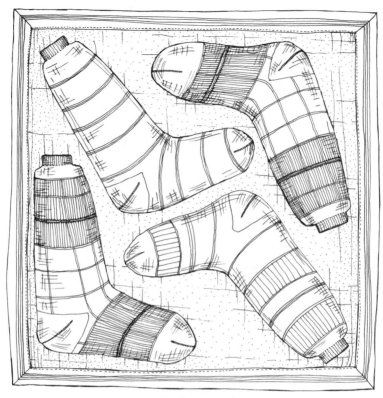

Sock pillow 4

To Make Pillow 4:

1. On base fabric, arrange socks in pleasing position.
2. Pin socks in final arrangement and stitch down with small hem stitches using standard sewing thread.
3. When all socks are in place, turn over fabric base and *carefully* slit small holes in fabric under socks with sharp scissors, being careful *not* to cut into sock.
4. Stuff each sock outline lightly with Dacron fiberfill, using a crochet hook or other blunt instrument to arrange filling.
5. Sew up slit with small hand stitches.
6. Pin 60-inch grosgrain ribbon around outside edge of fabric base and machine stitch in position with double row of stitching along inside edge of ribbon.
7. Measure completed pillow top and choose fabric in same dimension for pillow back. Finish pillow in knife-edge construction as described on page 25.

NINE

Quilting

QUILTING TECHNIQUES

Quilting is the technique of joining together two or more layers of fabric to create a new, stronger fabric. Quilt stitching, which is nothing more than the basic running stitch, has traditionally been used to enhance and strengthen patchwork and appliqué designs. It has also been used by itself to create intricate patterns of light and shadow on solid color cotton surfaces.

The most beautiful quilting is done by hand and although the technique is simple to learn, refining and controlling stitches over a large area such as a quilt can take years of practice. Accomplished quilters make stitches that are as tiny and evenly spaced on the underside of the fabric sandwich as they are on the top. Beginners will find it easy to make neat, even stitches on any fabric surface, but if the layers are dense it will be difficult to keep the stitches well formed on the back. Because of this, a pillow is ideal for a first quilt project. When the pillow is complete, only the surface of the stitching will show!

For fast, contemporary results, the sewing machine can be used, but be warned that the finished effect will be very different from quilting done by hand. Hand stitches are delicate and warm; machine stitching is bold and businesslike.

Although there is only one pillow included in this collection that has been done entirely with quilting, the quilting technique has been used to enhance many pillows in this book. The hexagon pillow on page 133, the camels for Peter on page 200 and the rice-sack pillow on page 134 all include quilt stitches. These pillows could have been completed without the addition of quilt stitching, but once added, the quilting has given visual unity as well as physical strength to the designs.

Where to Quilt

Quilt stitches will set off any area by creating shadows on the surface of the fabric. The thicker the layers the more dramatic (and the more difficult) the stitching.

When quilting patchwork or appliqué, set stitches parallel to the outside edge of a shape to emphasize a silhouette, quilt inside of an appliqué shape to add texture and volume. Quilt in the seams of a patchwork composition to create a soft effect. This unorthodox approach to quilting is not recommended for large projects such as a bed cover because quilting in patchwork seams will weaken the patchwork stitching. But Melanie Zwerling used it effectively to complete her hexagon pillow on page 133.

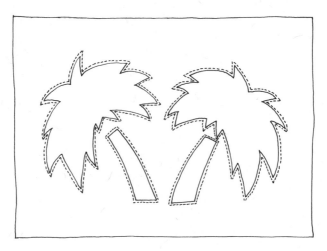

1. *Quilt parallel to the outside edge of a shape.*

*2. Quilt inside of an appliqué
shape to add texture
and volume.*

If you are quilting inside a large geometric patchwork area or on a large, solid color fabric, consider creating an independent image with quilt stitches, such as a simple circle, flower or other shape. Create an entire picture by defining shapes with quilting, such as the quilted house on page 184.

MATERIALS

Layers

A quilt project can be composed of two or three layers of fabric. For best results, the top and bottom layer should be a lightweight medium-weave cotton or cotton blend. The top layer can be a patchwork, appliqué, stenciled composition or a solid color fabric. Cotton printed with large simple shapes is also ideal for quilting because quilt stitches can be used to surround the major shapes, defining and enhancing any well-designed fabric.

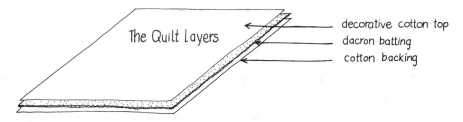

The Quilt Layers

decorative cotton top
dacron batting
cotton backing

Filling

Dacron batting, which comes in a large sheet, is ideal for the middle layer of a quilt sandwich.

Be sure to buy a good quality, soft filling meant for hand quilting because there are some less expensive varieties available that are wiry and stiff. Not only are those difficult to stitch, but they are unpleasant and harsh when layered between two pieces of lightweight fabric.

Quilt batting comes packaged in precut quilt sizes so read the labels carefully. An amount large enough for a full-size bed will be expensive but batting is also available in small amounts meant for baby quilts. This size package is ideal for beginning pillow quilters.

If Dacron quilt batting is not available, you may substitute soft flannel or muslin for the middle layer or eliminate the filling altogether, although the results will be less dramatic.

Quilt Fillings to Avoid

Do not use a foam sheet or coarse-feeling Dacron batting. They will be difficult to use and give unsatisfactory results. If you find you have purchased regular polyester or Dacron *fiberfill* meant for pillow filling (a common mistake), do not try to use it for a quilt unless you want to experiment with a contemporary approach. Use the Dacron for stuffing pillows, but look again for Dacron quilt *batting* "meant for filling quilts."

What Quilting Can Do

Quilting can add a gentle depth and texture to fabric as well as create a newer, stronger fabric from two or three weaker layers. The results, whether done by hand or machine, are soft and subtle. From across a room, quilting will contribute to the overall visual feeling of a piece of needlework, but it will not catch and hold your attention until seen at close range. Even as you quilt, the results will be so delicate and elusive that you may wonder why you are bothering to stitch. Yet, when you compare a piece of quilted needlework to the same composition unquilted, you will appreciate the extra depth and texture of the quilted piece. It is very much like adding a frame to a painting.

TRANSFERRING A PATTERN

Quilt by eye around the edge of a pattern as I did on the appliquéd vase of flowers on page 150 or transfer a pattern to the surface of a fabric. To do this, trace or draw your design to size on paper, pierce the lines of the design with a pin, tracing wheel or unthreaded sewing-machine needle and pin the perforated design onto the surface of your fabric. Use dress-maker's chalk in a color that will be visible on the fabric you have chosen and rub over the perforated holes until the marks are visible on the fabric. Remove the perforated design and quilt along the chalk lines. When the quilting has been completed, remove the chalk by brushing it off or dry cleaning. Or, prepare a drawing on paper, pin this to the fabrics being quilted and stitch through the paper. For more on this, see page 186.

PLACING THE LAYERS

Prepare the layers to be quilted so they are smooth and even and you will have accomplished half the job. Laying out materials for a large quilt can be tricky for a beginner but a small pillow top should be easy.

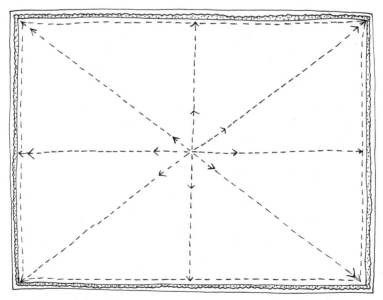

Baste all three layers firmly with a long running stitch before beginning to quilt. Work from the center out.

Iron all fabrics smoothly (batting will need no ironing) and lay out the backing fabric, face down, on a hard, flat area. Spread the interlining directly over this and smooth out any lumps or creases. Finally, place the decorative top or top to be decorated over the first 2 layers, face up. Make sure each layer is centered and free of wrinkles by placing your hand in the center of the material and working out any bulges toward the edge of the fabric. For safety, leave an extra margin of lining and backing sticking out from all sides of the top layer.

If you find that the fabrics shift uncontrollably as you add each new layer, consider taping the edges down with masking tape after each addition is in place.

Pinning and Basting

If you baste or pin the quilt layers together before beginning to stitch, you will be able to avoid bulges and fabric shifting, one of the biggest quilting pitfalls. For large quilt projects, it may be best to pin and then baste the layers, but for a small lap-sized quilt sandwich, pinning or basting alone may be sufficient.

Whichever you choose, be sure the layers are firmly fastened before you begin your actual quilt stitching. Always start from the center of the fabric and work toward the edges. When you feel sure that you have pinned the layers securely, you may begin to quilt. If the pins seem to be in the way as you work, you may have to consider basting. Baste through all 3 layers with long running stitches, again working from the center of the fabric outward, until you have firmly anchored the layers. Remove the pins. Later, as you quilt, remove the basting as it gets in the way.

THE QUILTING STITCH

Begin your quilting in the center of the composition and, wherever possible, work toward an outside edge. Thread your needle with a single strand the length of your arm and knot the end. Bring the needle up through the layers from the underside of the quilt sandwich to the top. When the thread is all the way through, give the knot a small tug to pull it past the backing fabric and into the lining. It takes practice to learn how much pressure to apply and in quilting for pillows, this procedure is done merely for practice if you intend to go on to a full-fledged bed cover. When the knot is in place, secure it with a backstitch and begin to quilt.

Expert quilters can make quilt stitches that are spaced every ⅟₁₆ inch, but only after years of practice. Beginners should do what feels comfortable (which will be about 5 or 6 stitches on the surface of the fabric, per inch).

Although the quilt stitch is just a running stitch, when several layers are involved the technique can be tricky. There are two methods to consider. First, make a running stitch in two separate strokes. With one hand, send the needle up through the layers at right angles to the surface, receive it on the top, pull it through and send it back down again on the same 90-degree angle. This is a reliable method but it can be annoyingly slow.

For faster results, make 2 or more stitches before pulling the needle through the fabric. Begin and end this procedure on the top layer of fabric and make sure you have caught all three layers on the needle before pulling it through. It will take care and practice to do this neatly and evenly.

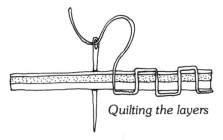

Quilting the layers

Quilting Aids: Thimble, Needle and Thread

There are a few tools that will help you as you quilt. Thimbles may seem unnecessary and they can feel awkward at first but after you poke yourself painfully with the point of the needle a few times, you will forgive it its drawbacks and appreciate the protection!

Use an in-between size 7-9 needle, which is delicate and pointed. The thimble will feel bulky and this tiny needle will feel almost nonexistent! Yet it will slip easily through the layers of your quilt sandwich and you will adjust to its size in no time.

Another aid is quilting thread, which is strong, heavily waxed and will resist almost all snags and knots. Quilting thread can be hard to find at local sewing supply counters but it is often available in needlework specialty shops and through mail-order catalogues (see page 212) in white and assorted colors.

For large projects, a quilting frame is useful, but lap-sized projects can be stitched easily without this aid. If you find that you do need the extra help of a frame, consider an embroidery hoop. For bulkier projects, use a quilting hoop, which is a more heavily constructed embroidery hoop, available also in needlwork shops and through the mail.

QUILTED HOUSE

This white-on-white pillow is fast and easy to stitch with a sewing machine but it can also be done by hand for a more traditional effect. The stitchery may look complicated, or even prohibitive, to first-time quilters, but with proper preparation it can be one of the easiest needlework pillows in this book.

Basic outline for quilted house

Materials Needed:

Finished size: 11 x 14 inches

Three pieces of muslin, each 11 x 14 inches (*plus seam allowance*)
Tracing paper or other lightweight paper
Sewing machine (optional—hand stitching may also be used)
Pillow stuffing

To Make This Pillow:

1. Iron all fabrics smooth.
2. Enlarge drawing shown here to appropriate size according to instructions on page 16. Transfer enlargement to tracing paper or other lightweight paper.

Outline for quilted house with extra stitching added

3. On a hard surface place 1 piece of muslin on top of another and smooth with the side of your hand.
4. Place drawing of house and trees directly on top of this and pin securely in place through both layers of fabric.
5. With long running stitches baste all 3 layers together. Remove pins.
6. Using white thread in your sewing machine needle and bobbin, set machine for 12–14 straight stitches per inch.
7. Starting on one side of the house, machine stitch along the lines of the drawing, through the paper and fabric. If you intend to duplicate this pillow, make a spare tracing and set it aside.
8. Wherever a line in the drawing stops, end off stitching and move the needle to the beginning of another line. Many areas such as the roof outline and window frames may be stitched with a continuous line, but there are some that will need to be stitched with separate lines.
9. When all lines are covered with stitching, gently pull away paper.
10. Add an extra row of stitching around each shape—the house, trees, lawn, cloud and smoke—about ⅛ inch inside each line already in place. Use the presser foot as a guide to put in the roof shingles. Stitch a line parallel to the top of the roof with the presser foot as a spacer. Add additional lines with the presser foot running parallel to the line before it.
11. Add vertical lines in roof by starting in center of roof and working out toward edge, also using presser foot as a guide. When one side is complete, go back to center and work toward remaining edge.
12. Using existing lines and the presser foot as a guide, put in additional stitches inside chimney, smoke, trees and next to the wavy line representing the lawn.
13. Finally, put in a single row of stitching around outside edge of muslin about ⅜ inch in from the edge of the fabric.
14. Finish pillow in knife-edge construction described on page 25, using muslin fabric or delicately printed cotton cut to 11 x 14 inches plus seam allowance.

TEN

Crazy Quilt

CRAZY-QUILT TECHNIQUES

Crazy quilting is a form of random appliqué in which pieces of fabric are overlapped to create a unified surface. Popular in the late 1800s, it was a great way to recycle worn-out but ornate fabrics into decorative throws for the parlor. Scraps from old clothing and linens cut in random shapes were stitched to a backing and held in place by embroidery stitching, which was often elaborate. The ''crazed'' surface that resulted became known as crazy quilting.

Today, scraps of velvet, silk and real wool are still expensive to buy and so transforming any scraps we might accumulate into crazy quilting still makes sense. For those many people filling their homes with Victorian-style furniture from antique shops, crazy quilting is a natural as an authentic decorative accent. As a craft, crazy quilting is great fun to do and it isn't hard to learn, even if you have little sewing experience. A quilt or comforter can be a time-consuming project and is better left until you have worked with some preliminary crazy quilting. As with all other new craft experiences, pillows are a great first project.

COLLECTING MATERIALS

Choose scraps of velvet and wool from old sewing projects as well as discarded neckties, scarves and clothing. Prepare neckties or articles of clothing by opening any seams and pressing fabric flat with a hot iron. Purchase small amounts of carefully selected wool to fill out your design, if needed, as I did for the crazy-quilt pillow on page 191. Challis, in a variety of patterns, is perfect for crazy quilting.

Also buy muslin for a base fabric. Since this backing will be completely covered by other materials, scrap muslin or old sheeting are both fine. It is best to use a solid color backing because it won't interfere with your "vision" as you arrange your patterned scraps on it. For easy stitching, lightweight fabric is best.

You will also need velvet, corduroy or other heavy-weight fabric for a pillow back. Sometimes it is best to wait until the pillow front is complete before deciding on a backing fabric. If you have a large piece left over from the crazy-quilt arrangement on the pillow front, this can often be ideal for the pillow back.

In addition, gather standard sewing supplies such as needle, thread, embroidery floss, scissors and a lot of straight pins.

PROCEDURE

Decide on the dimensions of your pillow and cut a muslin base to this size with at least ¼-inch seam allowance on all sides. Use dressmaker's carbon under the fabric and go over the shape of the pillow with a tracing wheel to mark the outline of the pillow on both sides of the muslin. You'll need the front side to guide you as you pin the fabric scraps and the back outline as a guide when doing the final pillow construction.

Choose a scrap of fabric roughly 2 x 2 inches and pin it onto the base fabric right side up. (This piece does not actually have to be 2 x 2 inches but keep your pieces large enough to be manageable.) Place a second piece of fabric in another pattern so at least one edge overlaps an edge of the fabric already in place, also right side up. (All pieces in crazy quilting are placed right side up.) The edge remaining on top where the two pieces overlap should be turned under and pinned with a ¼-inch hem. Continue adding pieces of wool or silk. The design choice is yours—just make sure the edges that sit on top in the final arrangement are turned under and securely pinned with a ¼-inch hem. The finished piece is meant to have a random appearance, but don't be afraid to change any fabric or alter any shape to improve the design.

Crazy-quilt procedure:

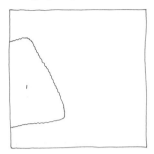

1. *Placement of first piece*

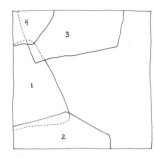

2. *Placement of additional pieces*

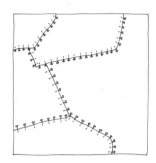

3. *Pinning under all edges that remain on top with ¼-inch hem*

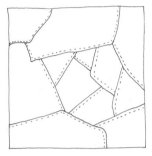

4. *Basting all pieces in place*

5. *Adding embroidery over all basted edges*

6. *(not shown) Complete pillow by sewing crazy-quilt top face to face with pillow back as described on page 25.*

Once all the pieces are securely pinned, baste everything in position. Using a single strand of thread in your needle, bring the needle up from the underside of the piece. Make running stitches that are short on the surface and long on the back. If you choose a thread color that blends well with as many of your crazy-quilt shapes as possible and make your stitches as described, the basting will be almost imperceptible. This is recommended because the basting is really permanent although it will be covered with decorative stitching later. Baste all edges securely, remove pins and press.

For a complete "look," all seams should be covered with decorative embroidery. Choose one stitch, such as the cross stitch or chain stitch, and carry it through the whole piece or work with an assortment of stitches. If you feel more comfortable with one particular embroidery stitch and intend to use it exclusively, consider varying the color of floss you use from seam to seam. Within a row of stitching you can even alternate colors, particularly with the cross stitch. The extra time it takes to change threads can be just enough to help give your stitching the variety and richness so important to crazy quilting. The interior of each patch may also be filled with decorative stitching. Mark the fabric using dressmaker's chalk with any shape you need to help keep your stitches even. A circle within a circle is a good jumping-off point for a daisy or other similarly shaped flower. A long straight line with two smaller lines jutting from it should be all you need to stitch a simple stem. For help with embroidery turn to page 49.

Once your decorative work is done, you are ready to convert your crazy quilting into a pillow. To do this, choose an appropriate heavy fabric for the backing and turn to basic pillow construction on page 25. If you wish to use a lightweight fabric as a pillow back, strengthen your choice with muslin (see page 85). For special, rounded Turkish corners, see instructions on page 29.

NEW DIRECTIONS FOR CRAZY QUILTING

Although I have described to you crazy quilting in its most familiar form, don't be afraid to experiment with it. For lighter looking crazy quilting particularly appropriate for a child's room, select flower-printed cotton fabrics as well as ginghams, dots and plaids. Complete as described above or use the zigzag stitch on your sewing machine for a quick and easy pillow. Ribbons also make great crazy quilting either neatly lined up or placed randomly. They may be stitched in place by hand with tiny running stitches or a machine straight stitch.

CRAZY-QUILT PILLOW

The first crazy-quilt pillow I owned was stitched by my sister-in-law Betsy and sent to me as a Christmas present. She had made a crazy-quilt bed cover out of old ties and scraps of velvets for her queen-sized bed. It took her what she describes as "forever" and when she finally finished it, she vowed she would never do it again. But the finished quilt was so beautiful and I oohed and aahed so consistently, that she finally decided to make me a pillow. When it arrived for Christmas, I was very excited and it immediately took a place of honor in our living room. It resided there for several years, where it did heavy service, being called upon to rest a weary head, arm or leg. But the poor pillow did not wear well. I'm not sure if it was an unlucky choice of particularly weak silks or whether silk ties in general are not strong enough to stand the demands of pillowdom. Whichever the reason, the slow deterioration of this pillow inspired me to make a new, stronger crazy-quilt pillow. This time, in addition to velvet scraps, I chose wool challis instead of silk. Some of the challis was from an old scarf, some from old ties and the rest left over from sewing projects (both mine and friends'). The only real problem I had in selecting material was having to reject some woven woolens because they were just too bulky—both visually and physically—to sit with the lightweight challis. Someday I hope to make a crazy-quilt pillow from these heavier fabrics, too. Because I used flowered challis and pale velvets, this crazy-quilt pillow is very lighthearted. The pillow I plan to make of plaid and striped wool will be more refined and sober. Decide which fits your own needs —and also which materials are available to you. If you decide on challis but don't have any in your scrap bag, consider buying ¼-yard swatches in a fabric shop. Although challis is very costly by the yard, a small amount of a few different patterns will go far in the world of crazy quilting. Try to ignore the grumbles of the salesperson, who will probably be annoyed by your request for such small amounts.

Crazy-quilt pillow

Materials Needed:

Finished size: 16 x 16 inches

One piece of muslin (or other lightweight, solid-color fabric), 16 x 16 inches (*plus seam allowance*)

Assortment of six or eight wool plaids, challis, velveteens and tweeds in small swatches. If you're making specific purchases, ¼ yard or less of each selection will be adequate, provided that there is enough to cover a 16 x 16-inch area.

Assortment of embroidery threads in colors that will be visible on solid-color swatches and along all seams

One piece of velveteen (or other heavy fabric), 16 x 16 inches (*plus seam allowance*)

Needle and thread

Sewing machine (optional)

Pillow stuffing

To Make This Pillow:

1. Pin a free-form piece of fabric from your material selection onto the surface of the muslin, right side up.
2. Place a second piece of another pattern so at least one edge overlaps an edge of the fabric already in place.
3. The edge remaining on top where the 2 pieces overlap should be turned under and pinned with a ¼-inch hem.
4. Continue adding pieces of challis or wool until the entire surface of muslin is covered. All pieces should be pinned in place and all raw edges remaining on top in the final arrangement should be turned under ¼ inch and hemmed.
5. Baste all edges down with a running stitch that is short on the surface of the crazy quilting and long on the back.
6. Cover all seams with decorative embroidery stitching using embroidery floss or pearl cotton. Use stitches shown on page 49 as a guide.
7. Add decorative embroidery inside any solid color fabric areas such as velveteen. Draw directly on these areas with pencil first, transfer tracing with graphite carbon or work freehand.
8. Complete the pillow in the knife-edge construction described on page 25. Add extra stitching to round the corners as described on page 29.

 **ELEVEN**

Stencil and Paint

STENCIL AND PAINT TECHNIQUES

The technique of making an image by applying paint through a cutout design, stencil has been most commonly used as decoration in the home on floors, furniture and walls, yet it is a process that also works well on fabric. Stenciled designs look especially striking on muslin and other solid color fabrics. Fabrics decorated with stencil look smashing made up into curtains, bed covers, table cloths and, of course, pillows. If you are looking for a pillow-decorating technique that's good looking, inexpensive and easy to do, try stencil. If you stencil on muslin or other soft fabric, take your project one step further and add quilting (see page 183). But first steps first.

Where to Begin

If this is a first experience for you with stencil, start slowly, as you would with anything else. You will find, happily, that once you get started you will be able to perfect your stencil technique quickly. A pillow top is an excellent first stencil project. It's a small, flat, contained surface. You

Materials for stencil:

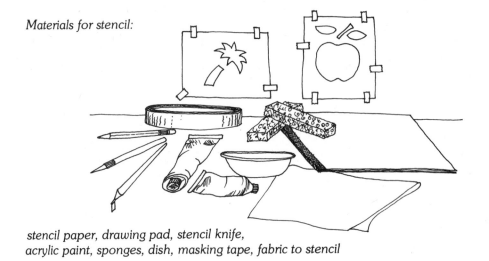

stencil paper, drawing pad, stencil knife,
acrylic paint, sponges, dish, masking tape, fabric to stencil

should get the knack of applying paint in just a few tries. If you make a few early mistakes, that's okay too. It's better to practice on a small, inexpensive square of muslin or old sheet than on a T-shirt or wall.

MATERIALS

Unbleached muslin is an ideal background fabric for a stenciled pillow. It's inexpensive and easy to find in local shops and it takes well to all sorts of design approaches. If you have a solid-color sheet that still has a good, strong, clean area left on it, you can use this too. A yard is all you need unless you plan something larger.

In addition to the fabric, you will also need drawing paper. Tracing paper or typing paper is fine but if your intended design is larger than the standard 8½ x 11 inches, try layout bond (sometimes called visualizing paper) from an art supply store. The paper should be slightly larger than the design you plan to stencil.

You will also need stencil paper, which is available in art supply stores. There are several types to choose from: oiled opaque board, waxed translucent board and heavy-weight acetate. Although all three work well, given a choice, I prefer the waxed translucent board. I find it the easiest to handle.

Also buy a number 11 X-acto or utility knife. If your design has a lot of curved edges, invest in a small swivel-bladed utility knife.

To apply paint to a small-to-medium-size area, you'll need a standard 5 x 7 x 1 inch kitchen sponge (which you will cut up later into small strips). You can also stencil with a short-bristled stiff paintbrush or spray paint, but I prefer the sponge method.

Half-inch masking tape and a stack of old newspapers are also necessary.

Acrylic paint is best for stencil because it's easy to use. Water-soluble when still wet, it dries into an impervious plastic washable surface. This paint is available in tubes and large jars in art supply stores in a wide range of colors. If you don't find exactly the colors you want, acrylic paint can be easily intermixed with itself for new colors. Do not mix acrylics with water colors, oil-base paint or anything other than acrylics. Paint has also begun to appear in variety stores that is packed in tiny plastic tubs and is sold as "fabric painting sets." These paints can also be used for stencil. Buying paint this way for big projects can be very expensive. On the other hand, if you are a beginner starting off on a small project, it might be a good investment. You will be paying for the luxury of an assortment of colors in small, easy-to-use containers. Once you go through this first set you will probably realize how easy and economical it is to put together your own set in larger amounts. The acrylic paint that comes in these tiny containers for fabric painting is exactly the same as the acrylic paint that comes in larger tubes or jars for use by artists.

CHOOSING A DESIGN

Choosing a design and preparing it for stencil can be the most intimidating part of the project. There is so much good picture source material, however, that even if you feel that you "can't draw" you should have no trouble creating a strong design. Once you realize that designs can be developed or even traced directly from a variety of places, it will simply become a matter of choosing *what* to stencil rather than figuring out *how* to do it. To me, choosing a design is like a trip to the candy store. There is so much to choose from that often it's hard to make a decision.

In addition to the designs in this book, there are many other books to look at for stencil ideas. Dover Publications has paperback collections of stencil designs including Early American, Pennsylvania Dutch, Victorian and Art Nouveau. These can be found in local bookstores and libraries, or write directly to Dover Publications, 180 Varick Street, New York, New York 10014, for a catalogue.

Whether you trace a stencil directly from a stencil source or develop your own design, think at first in terms of simple shapes and colors. Decide on the dimensions of your pillow front (don't forget to plan for seam allowance) and experiment with the placement of your design even if you are merely using a tracing from a book. Cut several pieces of layout paper to the exact dimensions of the intended pillow front and experiment with placement by tracing your design through onto these practice sheets. This kind of thinking and working will help your stencil to be a well-developed design rather than a half-developed idea.

Designs with More than One Color

Stencil is a primitive but very effective method of making and repeating an image on a surface. Successful stencil designs are simple, straightforward, basic shapes. One-color stencil designs are easy to do and can be very effective but multicolor designs can be very exciting and are not much harder to do.

Several colors can be applied through one stencil if the shapes are far enough apart and the stenciler works carefully. I used this method to do the stenciled camel pillows on page 200. For a more complicated design, where two or more colors overlap, you must make a separate stencil plate for each color. Generally, the paler colors or largest areas should go down first and the darker colors should be applied last. In some cases I have found it more expedient to stencil the large areas only and then add the delicate details with a paintbrush after the major areas have been stenciled.

In the case of fruit and leaf motifs, as shown on the following pages, the basic fruit and leaf shapes should be cut on one basic stencil plate.

The fruit should be stenciled in one basic color, with additional tones added freehand, as described on page 202. The stems and leaves should be carefully stenciled in a second color, also with details added later with a paintbrush.

Take care that you don't accidentally get the stem and leaf color into the area intended for the fruit.

If you don't feel comfortable about your skills with a paintbrush, use additional stencil plates to overlay colors.

PREPARING A STENCIL

Once you have prepared the actual design for stencil on paper, consider which method will be best for applying color. The next step is to prepare the actual stencil plates.

Registration Marks

If you are planning two or more plates on opaque stencil board, add three registration marks, such as small circular shapes, to the original drawing. Place them so they are well outside the area that includes the original design. Trace and cut these marks into each stencil plate and stencil into them too. When you have finished stenciling the first plate, you will be able to use these marks to line up additional ones. If you locate these marks cleverly in the original drawing, they will be well away from the actual drawing and you will be able to sew them into the seam allowance later when you assemble the pillow.

If you are using heavy-duty acetate or translucent board, you will be able to see clearly where you are placing your stencil, and unless your design is quite elaborate you will be able to work by eye.

Regardless of which type of board you are using for stencil, make sure to mark clearly which side of the stencil is front. I usually mark a big F in a conspicuous corner. Once you start stenciling, it's very easy to get confused. No amount of design registration marks or placement by eye will be effective if the plate is, in fact, used wrong side up.

Transferring the Design

If you are using opaque oiled board, place carbon paper between your drawing and the board. Tape your drawing securely to avoid shifting and transfer the design by tracing over it with a hard pencil or ballpoint pen.

Place the drawing and carbon so there are at least 2 inches all around the stencil design when it is cut. On the other hand, don't place a small design in the middle of a huge sheet of stencil paper and waste a lot of board. Instead, if you have a large board and a small- or medium-size design, measure the width of the design and decide what the best size of stencil board would be to accommodate the design comfortably. A design that measures approximately 8 x 8 inches should be centered on a board 12 x 12 inches.

Once you have completed the tracing, remove the carbon and the drawing. Place the stencil board (on which the tracing should now be clearly visible) on a stack of newspapers or other hard cutting surface. With a small utility knife, cut carefully around the outlines of the design. If you have a lot of straight lines in your design, use a ruler to help guide the blade. If there are a lot of curves, use a swivel blade as recommended on page 199.

If there is a second stencil plate planned for your design, transfer the design using the same method as plate 1. You can even trace right from the same drawing. Whereas you traced the basic flower and leaf shapes for plate 1, now trace the flower center and leaf veins for plate 2. Don't forget to trace the registration marks.

Applying the Paint

Once your stencil plates are cut, you are ready to apply paint through them. Wash and press the fabric to be stenciled, rule out the seam allowance as described on page 25 and lay it out flat, right side up, on a pile of newspapers. Tape the newspapers securely to the work surface and tape the corners of the fabric onto the newspaper. Lay the stencil plate in position on the fabric and tape this, too, in place.

Using acrylic paint, squeeze or spoon a small amount into a plastic dish or some other disposable receptacle. Even if you purchased the paint in a jar, always transfer a small amount to be used into a separate container so the unused portion will remain clean for a later time. Cut a strip about the size of a ladyfinger from an ordinary clean kitchen sponge and wet it in clean water. Firmly wring out all excess water so the sponge is dry but damp. Now, dip the tip of the sponge into the paint so it soaks in about ¼ inch. As you did with the water, wring the excess paint back into the container.

The secret of successful stenciling is to apply the paint slowly in thin layers. To make sure the sponge containing the paint is dry enough, dab the sponge several times on a clean sheet of newspaper. Once you are satisfied that any excess paint that could cause running or blotching has been dabbed off the sponge, you may begin to apply it to the stencil. By now, the sponge should be quite dry and as you dab it on the stencil it should leave a pale film inside the stencil shape. Make sure to dab carefully around the inside edges of the stencil shape as well as in the center of the cutout. After a few minutes the sponge will be so dry that you'll want to replenish the paint. Repeat the same cautious method as before. Dip it in paint, squeeze it out, dab it on newspaper and, finally, apply it to the stencil. This is a good time to experiment with color placement. Try dabbing more firmly around the edge of the stencil shape, leaving the center paler. For designs such as fruit, try applying the paint more heavily on one side only.

After two coats of paint you may feel that the stenciled shapes are dark enough. If the stencil is firmly taped along one edge, remove the tape on the other edges and peek. Lift the stencil gently and be sure not to wiggle the stencil plate. If you want to add more paint, it is important to keep the plate aligned with what you have already done.

If you feel that you still need more paint, continue the stencil process slowly until you build up to the color depth you want. When you are satisfied, give the paint a few minutes to dry. This shouldn't take more than a few minutes since acrylics dry very quickly. Now, peel away the masking tape and remove the stencil plate carefully. Give the design another few minutes to dry before you begin with the next plate, if there is one.

When the stencil work is completed and dry, choose an appropriate fabric for a pillow back and assemble, according to instructions beginning on page 25. You may choose to use the same fabric as the front for the backing or experiment with a contrasting or patterned material.

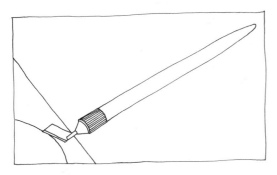

Cutting a curved-edge stencil with a swivel-blade utility knife

Applying paint with a sponge through a stencil

CAMELS FOR PETER

The stenciled camels were done as a gift for my brother Peter, who collects camel motifs. His collection ranged from camel postcards to carved camels. It now includes camel pillows.

These pillows, like many in this book, were made of leftovers from sewing projects. The basic material was unbleached muslin. Since there was only enough muslin for the three pillow fronts, I chose a backing material of off-white cotton fabric sprigged with pale flowers.

I worked first on layout paper (see page 194) designing the camels, mosque and palm trees. I wanted the finished pillows to be seen as a continuous view to suggest the desert and I wanted the pillow placement to be interchangeable. After a lot of thought and rough sketching, I finally decided on one pillow with a mosque bordered by palm trees and two pillows with a man leading a camel bordered by the same palm trees. The pillows would have a unifying ground plane to represent the sand. Each pillow works well alone also.

Materials Needed:

Finished size of each pillow: 11 x 14 inches

Nine pieces of muslin 11 x 14 inches (*plus seam allowance*)
Three pieces of Dacron quilt batting cut to same size
Masking tape
Two sheets of translucent stencil paper measuring 11 x 14 inches each.
    (If translucent paper is not available, use opaque stencil paper. Use carbon paper to transfer design to surface of this type. Heavy-gauge acetate may also be substituted.)
Heavy cardboard or stack of newspapers for cutting surface
Swivel-blade utility knife (available in hardware stores)
Acrylic paint in colors shown in drawings
Plastic egg tray or other disposable plastic tray for mixing paint
Small new kitchen sponge cut into strips
Jar of water
White quilting thread (white bel-waxed thread may be substituted) and small sewing needle
Sewing machine (optional—for final pillow construction)
Pillow stuffing

Note: The three pillows that follow are all the same size. Use one of the motifs twice to create three pillows.

Camels for Peter

To Make These Pillows:

1. Remove 3 pieces of muslin from group and set other materials aside.
2. Enlarge drawings shown here to the appropriate size as directed on page 16.
3. Tape drawings (one at a time) to hard surface and tape translucent paper directly on top.
4. With hard pencil, trace stencil outline onto stencil paper. (If using opaque paper, use carbon paper for transferring design.)
5. Remove artwork and store for future use. Tape stencil to cutting surface. Using swivel-blade utility knife (shown on page 199), carefully cut out each shape.
6. Transfer and cut second piece of artwork using same method.
7. Mix a small amount of pink and purple acrylic paint in one section of egg tray for the mosque. All other areas may be stenciled with

paint straight from the tube: raw umber for camels, ochre for the man, dark green for palm leaves and raw ochre for palm trunk. Use ochre, umber and white, in that order, for sand areas.

8. Following directions on page 198 for applying paint, stencil in sand areas in the order listed in step 7.

9. Stencil other colors, one at a time, as listed above. Complete all 3 pillow tops.

10. When paint is dry (approximately 5 minutes), add quilting.

11. Layer each stenciled top with quilt batting and muslin backing in order shown on page 179.

12. Smooth, pin and baste together.

13. Put small quilt stitches (page 183) around each major shape, as shown in drawing.

14. Complete pillows in knife-edge construction described on page 25 using muslin or other fabric cut to size.

FRUIT PILLOWS ON VELVET

The fruit pillows were stenciled on velvet, again using acrylic paint. I only made one of each pillow, although I had gone to the trouble of cutting stencils for each. Ideally, if one takes the time to prepare a stencil, it should be used more than once. Otherwise, why not just draw the picture directly onto the fabric? I found that if I worked out the drawing carefully and transferred it to a stencil, I would be more assured of creating a pleasing design, and since I was using expensive velvet, I didn't want to make any mistakes. In addition, having the cut stencil gives me the option of using it again.

To do the design I needed pictures for reference. For this I used reproductions of old fruit prints. First, I scaled the drawings up (see page 16). In the process of enlarging them, I also simplified and separated the shapes to make them appropriate for stencil. Where a leaf over-lapped a stem, I would close off each shape, leaving a small bridge. As with the camel pillows, the shapes of the fruit and leaves were isolated enough from each other without color overlaps so that I needed to cut only one stencil plate for each design. The color variations on the surface of the fruit and leaves I intended to make freehand by applying the sponge within the large stencil shapes. For example, on the peach pillow, first I stenciled the leaves pale yellow ochre. When the yellow ochre was dry, I stenciled a thin coat of green around the edge of the shape, leaving the leaf centers pure ochre but tinting the edges slightly darker. On the peaches themselves, first I stenciled peachy yellow. Then I carefully added dabs of brown, light pink and dark pink to create shading. All the time the peach stencil remained in position, so each new color addition would be stopped by the outside edge of the stencil. The veining of the leaves I did last by hand with a paintbrush. Although I hadn't much experience with this type of painting, I found that if I kept the original print nearby for reference as I worked, it helped me know where to make my marks and it acted as a guide to light and dark color changes. The results are primitive, but effective.

Materials Needed:

Finished size of each pillow: 14 x 14 inches

Masking tape
Two sheets of translucent stencil paper measuring 14 x 14 inches each. (If translucent paper is not available, use opaque stencil paper. Use carbon paper to transfer design to surface of this type. Heavy-gauge acetate may also be substituted.)
Heavy cardboard or stack of newspapers for cutting surface
Swivel-blade utility knife (available in hardware stores)
Plastic egg tray or other disposable plastic tray for mixing paint
Small new kitchen sponge cut into strips
Jar of water
Four pieces of velveteen measuring 14 x 14 inches (*plus seam allowances*)
For the peach pillow, acrylic paint in the following colors: brown, pale yellow, green, ochre, deep peach
For the apple pillow, acrylic paint in the following colors: brown, chartreuse, soft pink, medium green, dark green
Small pointed paintbrush
Sewing machine (optional)
Pillow stuffing

To Make These Pillows:

1. Enlarge drawings given here to appropriate size using method described on page 16.
2. Transfer drawings to stencil paper and cut out stencils as described on page 197.

3. To stencil the peach, tape stencil in place with masking tape, as shown earlier.
4. Apply acrylic paint with a sponge as described earlier.
5. When stenciling is complete, add veining in leaves by eye, with paintbrush.

Basic stencil for peach pillow

6. Stencil apple design using sponge for large areas and paintbrush for large veins.
7. Complete pillows in knife-edge construction described on page 25 using velveteen as pillow back.

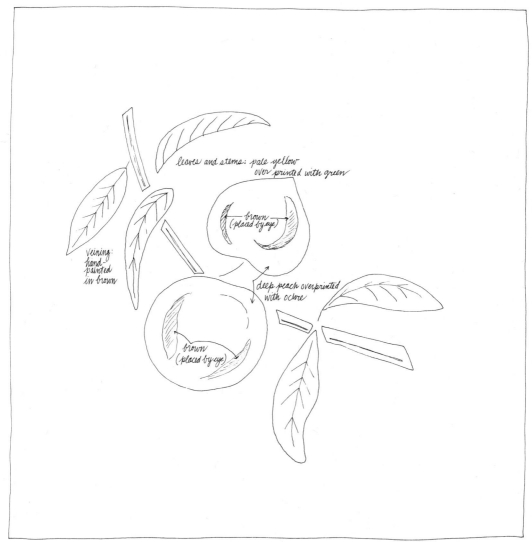

Peach pillow with freehand color additions as described on page 202

Basic stencil for apple pillow

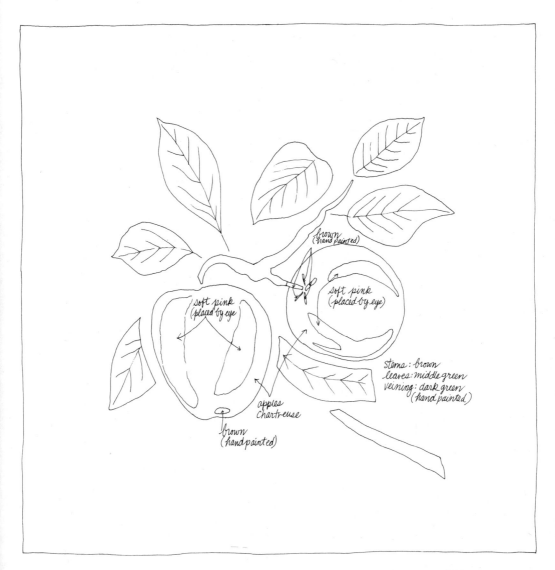

Apple pillow with freehand color additions as described on page 202

STAR PILLOW

The inspiration for Barbara Barnett's wonderful star pillows was her husband David. Every Valentine's Day she gives him a very special needlework present; in 1976 she decided to give him "the moon and stars." The finished quilted and stuffed pillows—soft sculpture really—were so successful that one of the star pillows presented here was displayed by the Cooper-Hewitt Museum in New York City as part of the star-motif section in their opening exhibit. Here is a step-by-step description of how to make your own star using fine white muslin, quilt stitching and acrylic paint.

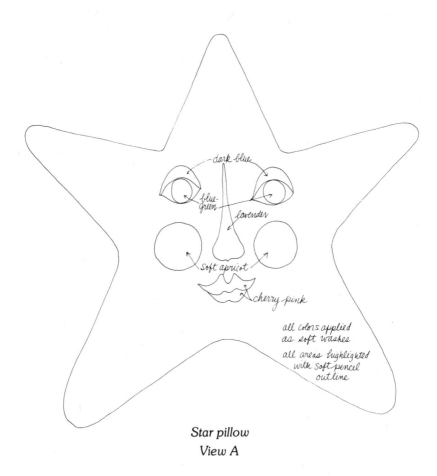

Star pillow
View A

Materials Needed:

Muslin for pillow front and back (in amounts appropriate to your pillow
   size)
Acrylic paints or other permanent dyes in colors shown
Needle and quilting thread (or bel-waxed cotton)
Sewing machine (optional)
Pillow stuffing

To Make This Pillow:

1. First trace and enlarge the star (view A) to the appropriate size as
    described on page 16. Barbara's larger star (shown in the color
    section) measures 10½ inches across the top points, but she also
    made several smaller ones, so choose a size that appeals to you.
2. Fold the tracing of the star in half lengthwise and trace on a separate
    piece of paper half the nose and half the star as shown in view B.
    Add ¼-inch seam allowance all around. This is the front pattern.
3. Make the back pattern by tracing around half the star pattern again
    (excluding the nose) and adding ¼-inch seam allowance (view C).
4. Cut out two fronts and two backs by tracing each pattern twice onto
    the wrong side of the muslin. Use dressmaker's carbon and a tracing
    wheel or hard pencil to do this or merely trace pattern through
    muslin with a pencil.
5. Stitch the two fronts together along the center seam by placing *right
    sides* face to face. Align to the noses according to the pin method
    described on page 123.
6. When the stitching is complete, clip the seam allowance around the
    nose to ease the fabric tension and press the seam open. Stuff the
    nose with small pieces of fabric to make the job easier.
7. Stitch the backs together down the center seam. Place right sides
    together and align with pins. Stitch down this seam but leave a 3- to
    4-inch opening in the center for final pillow stuffing. When the back
    panel is stitched, put it aside.
8. Next, transfer the star face features to the front. Place the full face
    pattern (view A) on the right side of the fabric. Place carbon in
    between, carbon side facing the fabric. Outline eyes, nose, lips and
    cheeks, making dots, which are easier to cover with quilt stitching
    than solid lines. Do right side of face, then left side, folding nose
    each time in the opposite direction.

9. Prepare for quilting and stuffing by cutting a piece of muslin large enough to lay under the completed star front. Baste this to the wrong side of star face, using long running stitches. Be sure to smooth out any wrinkles or bulges before you begin work and to baste around all star points.
10. Stitch around eyes, nose, lips and cheeks, using a tiny hand running stitch described on page 183. For best results, use white quilting thread or bel-waxed cotton thread.
11. When all areas are defined with quilt stitching, use a small pair of scissors and carefully slit muslin backing in the appropriate areas to be stuffed—inside the nose, the cheeks, the lips and the eyes. Take special care to cut the backing only. Do not cut into the front fabric!
12. Gently stuff small amounts of fiberfill into the stitched areas, using a knitting needle or other gently pointed instrument to guide the stuffing into the hard-to-reach areas. Use stuffing with moderation. If the features are too tightly packed, the fabric will bulge and the stitching will be strained. All stuffing should be soft, gently reflecting light.

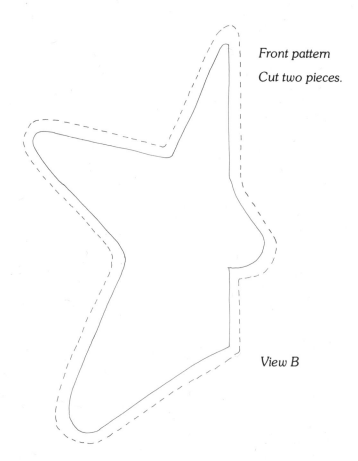

Front pattern

Cut two pieces.

View B

When all areas are stuffed, stitch all slits closed with hand stitches.

13. Join the front and back panels by placing them together, *right sides together*, and stitching around the outside outline, leaving enough of an opening to reverse the pillow. Clip carefully into seam allowance, reverse pillow and stuff with fiberfill. Stitch the back opening closed.

14. To add color to the face, treat areas to be painted with a coat of polymer medium, a water-soluble acrylic liquid available in art supply stores. Apply with a paintbrush. Once dry, this medium is a permanent plastic and it will prevent paint applied directly on it from bleeding. (Be sure to wash the brush you have used immediately after use. Polymer medium dries quickly—and permanently.) When the polymer medium is completely dry on the pillow fabric (about 5 minutes), use watered-down acrylic paint, Doctor Martin's Dyes or permanent ink to add pale colors to the face of the star. Experiment on a piece of scrap muslin until you are comfortable with the paint or dye.

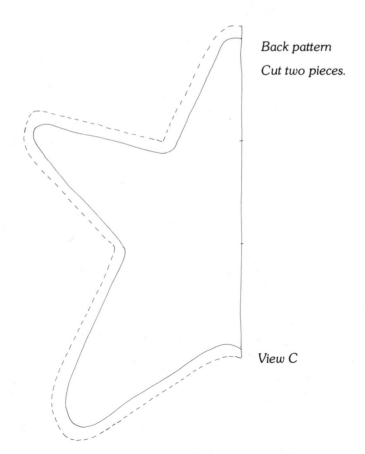

Back pattern

Cut two pieces.

View C

Supplies Through the Mail

It's always more fun and infinitely more inspiring to shop for materials and supplies in stores where you can see and feel what you are buying. Craft needlework stores, yard goods shops and department stores are now so spread across the country that you should be able to find almost any supply you need close to home. If, however, you have trouble locating certain, often elusive, items such as quilting thread or hardanger cloth (for cross stitch) check the following mail-order firms, which have competitively priced, well-stocked catalogues.

Herrschners, Inc.
Stevens Point, Wisconsin 54481

Lee Wards
840 North State Street
Elgin, Illinois 60120

Bibliography

Books and magazines are often the best source of inspiration for pillow ideas. The following list includes books that I have found invaluable to my own pillow stitchery. All are available at bookstores and local libraries.

Embroidery, Cross Stitch and Needlepoint:

Ambuter, Carolyn. *Carolyn Ambuter's Complete Book of Needlepoint*. New York: Workman Publishing Company, 1972.

de Dillmont, Thérèse. *Encyclopedia of Needlework*. Philadelphia: Running Press, reprint, no date.

Gartner, Louis J., Jr. *Needlepoint Design*. New York: William Morrow and Company, Inc., 1970.

Jones, Mary Eirwen. *English Crewel Designs*. New York: William Morrow and Company, 1974.

Thomas, Mary. *Mary Thomas' Embroidery Book*. New York: Gramercy Publishing Company, reprint from 1936.

213

Patchwork, Appliqué, Quilting and Crazy Quilting:

Edwards, Phoebe. *The Mountain Mist Blue Book of Quilts.* Cincinnati, Ohio: Stearns and Foster, no date.

Holstein, Jonathan. *The Pieced Quilt.* New York: Galahad Books, 1973.

Ickis, Marguerite. *The Standard Book of Quiltmaking and Collecting.* New York: Dover Publications, 1959.

Jarnow, Jill. *The Patchwork Point of View.* New York: Simon and Schuster, 1975.

Lane, Rose Wilder. *The Woman's Day Book of American Needlework.* New York: Simon and Schuster, 1963.

Stencil:

Day, JoAnne C. *The Complete Book of Stencilcraft.* New York: Simon and Schuster, 1974.

Jarnow, Jill. *(Re)Do It Yourself.* New York: The Dial Press, 1977.

Waring, Janet. *Early American Stencils on Walls and Furniture.* New York: Dover Publications, reprint, 1968.